Excel

Get the Results You Want!

Years 5–6
Selective Schools and Scholarship Reading Tests

Alan Horsfield

PASCAL
PRESS

© 2022 Alan Horsfield and Pascal Press

Completely new edition incorporating late 2020 Selective School test changes

Reprinted 2024

The publisher wishes to thank Kristine Brown for her permission to use part of her introduction in this book.

ISBN 978 1 74125 631 4

Pascal Press Pty Ltd
PO Box 250
Glebe NSW 2037
(02) 9198 1748
www.pascalpress.com.au

Publisher: Vivienne Joannou
Project editor: Mark Dixon
Edited by Rosemary Peers
Proofread by Mark Dixon
Answers checked by Dale Little
Cover by DiZign Pty Ltd
Typeset by Grizzly Graphics (Leanne Richters) and lj Design (Julianne Billington)
Printed by Vivar Printing/Green Giant Press

Contents

Mini tests

Sample tests

Answers

ABOUT THIS BOOK

The first section includes 48 Mini Reading Tests with five different types of tests. These reflect the format of the four subsections in the NSW Selective High School Placement Test:

- One text
- Two texts
- Poetry
- Cloze exercises
- Comparing four texts.

The second section includes two Sample Tests. These are based on the Selective School Reading Test. Each test has been carefully constructed to reflect the length, format and level of the actual test.

BACKGROUND TO SELECTIVE TESTING

Tests for entry into selective government schools were introduced in order to provide an opportunity for pupils with scholastic aptitude. Over 15 000 applications are made for the just over 4000 selective places available and entry is quite competitive. It is not unusual for some primary schools not to be able to place even one of their pupils into a selective school.

The tests were updated in 2020 with a greater emphasis on literacy, critical-thinking skills, mathematical reasoning and problem solving. The General Ability Test has been replaced by a Thinking Skills Test. The new NSW Selective High School Placement Test adjusts and balances the weighting given to the Reading, Thinking Skills, Mathematical Reasoning and Writing components. These changes were in response to the findings of the 2018 Review of Selective Education Access report, commissioned by the NSW Department of Education.

ABOUT THE SELECTIVE SCHOOL TEST

The NSW Selective High School Placement Test consists of four sections:

- **Reading** (30 questions in 40 minutes)
- **Thinking Skills** (40 questions in 40 minutes)
- **Mathematical Reasoning** (35 questions in 40 minutes)
- **Writing** (one question in 30 minutes).

The tests, except Writing, are in multiple-choice form, with each question being of equal value. Marks are awarded for each correct answer and applicants are advised to guess the answer if they are uncertain.

Although there are similarities in the content of the NSW Selective High School Placement Test and the ACER Scholarship Tests, since the Selective Schools Test format changed in 2020 there are now more differences.

HOW THE RESULTS ARE USED BY PUBLIC SCHOOLS

Entry to selective high schools is based on academic merit. In 2022 changes were made to the allocation of places. Under the Equity Placement Model, up to 20% of places are held for members of the following disadvantaged and under-represented groups:

- students from low socio-educational advantage backgrounds
- First Nations students
- rural and remote students
- students with disability.

It is important to remember that the places allocated under the Equity Placement Model will not necessarily be filled. In 2023, the first year of this new system, less than 10% of these places were offered. This means that more than 90% of the places were offered to general applicants. The new system has helped close the educational gap in participation from disadvantaged groups without having a significant impact on other applicants.

Students no longer receive a test score or placement rank. The new performance report will instead place students in one of the following categories:

- top 10% of candidates
- next 15% of candidates
- next 25% of candidates
- lowest 50% of candidates.

This change addresses privacy and wellbeing concerns including unhealthy competition between students. The sole purpose of the test is to identify students who would benefit from the chance to study at a selective school and, since it doesn't test knowledge of the curriculum, there is no diagnostic merit in the test—unlike the NAPLAN test, which can help identify areas where children can improve.

Minimum entry scores for selective schools are no longer published because these change from year to year and depend on the number of applicants, their relative performance and the number of families who decline an offer. Students placed on the reserve list no longer receive a numerical rank; instead an indication of how long it will take to receive an offer, based on previous years, is provided.

A selection committee for each selective high school decides which students are to be offered places. These committees also decide how many students are to be placed on the reserve list. Should a student with a confirmed offer turn down a place at a selective school, the place will be offered to the first student on the reserve list.

There is an appeals panel for illness or other mitigating circumstances. All applicants are advised of the outcome. The NSW Government provides detailed information on the application and selection process for parents on the Selective High School Placement Test. This is available from: https://education.nsw.gov.au/parents-and-carers/learning/tests-and-exams/selective-school-test. Sample test papers are also available on this website.

ABOUT THE SCHOLARSHIP TESTS

The ACER Scholarship Tests, which are usually held around May, are coordinated by the Australian Council for Educational Research (ACER). This testing is for entry to around 200 independent schools. About 15 000 students throughout Australia sit these tests. The tests cover three levels:

- Level 1: the last year of primary school (Year 6)
- Level 2: the second year of high school (Year 8)
- Level 3: Year 10 in high school.

Each private school awards its own scholarships. You can put your name down for more than one school but you will need a special registration form. There is also a separate fee for each school and you lodge your registration directly with the school and not with ACER.

You may be limited in the number of schools to which you can apply. This might happen if a school insists you have to take the test at their testing centre. Candidates usually take the exam at the school which is their first choice. There are exceptions for country and interstate candidates.

The ACER Scholarship Tests comprise:

- Test 1: Written Expression (25 minutes)
- Test 2: Humanities—Comprehension and Interpretation (40 minutes)
- Test 3: Mathematics (40 minutes)
- Test 4: Written Expression (25 minutes).

HOW THE RESULTS ARE USED BY PRIVATE SCHOOLS

The results are used by private schools to select students who have applied for a scholarship. Typically the highest scorers are considered first, together with any additional background information that might have been provided. It is important therefore to provide as much detail as possible in the application form to assist the selection committee in deciding between pupils who may have similar scores.

ABOUT THE READING TEST

The NSW Selective High School Placement Test and all scholarship tests include a Reading comprehension component that asks you to read a number of texts and then answer questions to show how well you understood them.

The NSW Selective High School Placement Test calls this section Reading. The ACER Scholarship Tests call it Humanities—Comprehension and Interpretation.

The question format for the Selective School Test varies from subsection to subsection. At the time of writing, the question format is as follows for the four subsections:

- Literary prose text—multiple-choice questions about two different texts or about different stages of one text.
- Poetry—multiple-choice questions about one poem.
- Factual text—a task which asks you to place sentences or phrases into an information text in a way that makes sense (a cloze task).
- Varied short texts—matching descriptive statements to four short texts on the same theme but with different content and written in different styles or from different perspectives.

ADVICE TO STUDENTS

The tests are difficult and you may not finish them in the time available. Don't worry about this because many students will also find the questions very hard. You can't learn the answers to the questions in these tests like you can with some school tests because they force you to deal with new situations.

We wish you all the best in the tests and hope these notes will be of some help in making you familiar with the different types of questions in the test and helping you increase your speed and accuracy. Don't worry if you don't get a place

because there are thousands and thousands of applicants. Just give it your best shot.

Here is a summary of the advice that the Education Department and ACER give to people taking the tests:

- There is nothing special that you have to learn in order to do these tests.
- These are tests to see whether you can think clearly with words and numbers.
- Listen carefully to the instructions.
- If you are not sure what to do then ask.
- Make sure you know where to mark the answers for each test.
- Do not open the test booklet until you are told.
- Read each question carefully before giving your answer.
- There is no penalty for guessing—so guess if you are not sure.
- Don't rush—work steadily and as carefully as you can.
- If a question is too hard, don't worry—come back to it later if you have time.
- It is easy to get your answers out of order, so always check the number of the question you are answering.
- Every now and then make sure the answer is in the correctly numbered circle.
- Feel free to write on the question booklet for any rough working.
- Don't do any rough work on the answer sheet.
- If you want to change an answer, rub it out and fill in the appropriate circle for your new answer.
- Keep track of the time—you will not be told when time is running out.
- Don't fold the answer sheet—it has to be put through a machine to mark it.

Reading answer sheet

Mark your answers here.

To answer each question, fill in the appropriate circle for your chosen answer.

Use a pencil. If you make a mistake or change your mind, erase and try again.

You can make extra copies of this answer sheet to mark your answers to the two Sample Reading Tests in this book.

1 A B C D ○○○○	11 A B C D ○○○○	21 A B C D ○○○○
2 A B C D ○○○○	12 A B C D ○○○○	22 A B C D ○○○○
3 A B C D ○○○○	13 A B C D ○○○○	23 A B C D ○○○○
4 A B C D ○○○○	14 A B C D ○○○○	24 A B C D ○○○○
5 A B C D ○○○○	15 A B C D E F G ○○○○○○○	25 A B C D ○○○○
6 A B C D ○○○○	16 A B C D E F G ○○○○○○○	26 A B C D ○○○○
7 A B C D ○○○○	17 A B C D E F G ○○○○○○○	27 A B C D ○○○○
8 A B C D ○○○○	18 A B C D E F G ○○○○○○○	28 A B C D ○○○○
9 A B C D ○○○○	19 A B C D E F G ○○○○○○○	29 A B C D ○○○○
10 A B C D ○○○○	20 A B C D E F G ○○○○○○○	30 A B C D ○○○○

MINI TEST 1: Narrative

Read the text below then answer the questions.

Urashima the Fisher

A long time ago, on the coast of Japan, there lived a family of fisherfolk named Kuzumi. The youngest boy was called Urashima. He was a kind boy and a clever fisherman.

One day he went out in his boat and threw out his line. He didn't catch any fish—instead he caught a great tortoise. It had a large hard shell, a funny wrinkled old-man face and a tiny tail. Now, although its face looked old, this tortoise was only a youngster. Urashima, too, knew that the tortoise was no older than he; and he also knew that Japanese tortoises lived for a thousand years. So, he thought to himself, 'Why should I kill it, when there are plenty of fish for me to eat? After all, it's got about another nine hundred and eighty-eight years to live yet. It would be cruel to kill it now.' So Urashima threw the tortoise back into the sea and went on fishing.

After he made his catch he fell drowsy. So he lay down in his boat in the hot summer sun and went off to sleep. As he slept a beautiful girl came up from beneath the waves. She climbed into the boat and woke Urashima with a touch of her hand. He stared at her still dazed with sleep.

'I am the daughter of the Sea God,' she said, 'and I live in the Dragon Palace beyond the sea. I was the tortoise you threw back, for my father sent me in disguise to see what you would do. Now my father has sent for you. If you learn to love me, we shall be married and live in happiness for a thousand years in the Dragon Palace.'

Adapted by Noela Young, *NSW School Magazine,* May 1994

For questions **1–6**, choose the option (**A**, **B**, **C** or **D**) which you think best answers the question.

1 Urashima Kuzumi was the
A father of the Kuzumi family.
B only child of the Kuzumi family.
C youngest child of the Kuzumi family.
D beautiful daughter of the Kuzumi family.

2 The word 'drowsy' is closest in meaning to
A weary.
B sleepy.
C droopy.
D exhausted.

3 The tortoise was
A about eighty years old.
B one thousand years old.
C less than twenty years old.
D nine hundred and eighty-eight years old.

4 Urashima let the tortoise go because it
A wasn't a fish.
B was too tough to eat.
C was too big for the boat.
D still had many years to live.

5 The tortoise was caught on Urashima's line
A by accident.
B as planned by the Sea God.
C because it was not very fast.
D because Urashima was a clever fisherman.

6 The Sea God's daughter climbed into Urashima's boat because she
A was afraid of sea creatures.
B was exhausted from swimming.
C wanted a ride back to the coast.
D wanted to reward Urashima for his kindness.

Read the text below then answer the questions.

Preparation time: 20 minutes
Cooking time: 17 minutes

Recipes have been tested in a 650-watt microwave oven. If your oven is 500 watts, increase cooking times by 20% (12 seconds for each minute); if 700 watts, reduce cooking time by 5%.

Front of recipe card

Potatoes Anna   Serves 4

Preparation time: 20 minutes
Cooking time: 17 minutes
750 grams Packer's Pick Potatoes—peeled and thinly sliced
90 grams butter—melted
2 rashers bacon—finely chopped
1/2 teaspoon finely ground white pepper
1. Place thinly-sliced potatoes in a bowl, cover with cold water and allow to stand for 10 minutes. Drain potatoes and dry completely with a towel.
2. Arrange potato slices evenly in a 1.5 litre capacity microwave ring dish, pour melted butter over the top, sprinkle with chopped bacon and dust with pepper.
3. Place a sheet of paper towel loosely over the top and microwave on High 100% power for 15 minutes.
4. Allow Potatoes Anna to stand for 2 minutes before removing paper and serving.
Serving Suggestions: Potatoes Anna are particularly delicious served as a vegetable accompaniment to steamed and baked fish.
Tip: Food placed in a ring formation cooks more evenly in a microwave oven.

For the best results, use the best potatoes—Packer's Pick

Back of recipe card

For questions **1–7**, choose the option (**A**, **B**, **C** or **D**) which you think best answers the question.

1 Potatoes Anna is best served with
  A bacon.
  B melted butter.
  C steamed fish.
  D Packer's Pick potatoes.

2 In the recipe the word 'dust' means
  A fine dirt.
  B brush off.
  C fine powder.
  D sprinkle with.

3 To make sufficient Potatoes Anna for 6 people I would need an extra
  A 2 rashers of bacon.
  B 1 rasher of bacon.
  C 4 rashers of bacon.
  D 6 rashers of bacon.

4 A person preparing Potatoes Anna does not require
  A salt.   **B** water.   **B** butter.   **D** pepper.

5 In a 650-watt microwave oven, actual cooking time in the oven will be
  A less than 15 minutes.
  B 15 minutes.
  C 17 minutes.
  D more than 17 minutes.

6 From the start of preparation until it is ready to eat, Potatoes Anna requires
  A 17 minutes.
  B 20 minutes.
  C 37 minutes.
  D 39 minutes.

7 For evenly cooked Potatoes Anna,
  A use only the best potatoes.
  B cook a little longer than suggested.
  C arrange food in a ring formation before microwaving.
  D allow potatoes to stand for two minutes before serving.

Read the text below then answer the questions.

Buying men's t-shirts

You can tell a lot about a person by the T-shirt they wear—including where they have holidayed.
These T-shirts come in many styles and all sizes.

Bold and Basic

This basic T-shirt features a relaxed fit that is also loved by the younger female. Made from 100% cotton, this T-shirt is both durable and soft—a great combination!

$46

Trip Advisor

Enjoy the feel of a fine weave. It's one of the nation's best shirts made from durable polyester. Medium weight for comfort! Customise the front with your own graphic and let others see where you have been!

$42

Summer Sizzler

Sleeveless T-shirts and tanks help cool you down because they allow for air to flow—the key to keeping cool in summer. They're also a great way to layer in cool weather, without overheating. Useful as a cotton undershirt.

$49

Cool and Casual

Comfortable, casual and loose fitting, our collared heavyweight T-shirt will become a favourite. Made from pre-shrunk 100% cotton, it looks good on the young man. Double-stitched hems for extra durability— and an accessible price .

$38

For questions **1–6**, choose the option (**A**, **B**, **C** or **D**) which you think best answers the question.

1   Not being able to spend over $40 on a T-shirt, my only option would be
A Bold and Basic.
B Trip Advisor.
C Summer Sizzler.
D Cool and Casual.

2   The name 'Bold and Basic' uses an example of
A alliteration.
B hyperbole (exaggeration).
C synonyms.
D personification.

3   If I preferred a T-shirt that was **not** made from cotton, I could choose
A Bold and Basic.
B Trip Advisor.
C Summer Sizzler.
D Cool and Casual.

4   The phrase 'accessible price' (Cool and Casual) means
A a discount price.
B the purchase price.
C a price many people can afford.
D the price of the cheapest T-shirt available.

5   Which T-shirt has a style that may be suitable for both men and women?
A Bold and Basic
B Trip Advisor
C Summer Sizzler
D Cool and Casual

6   Which of these is a feature of Summer Sizzler?
A a wide collar with a buttoned V-front
B doubles as an undershirt in cool weather
C personal graphic on the front
D doubled-stitched hem for improved durability

MINI TEST 4: Information report

Read the text below then answer the questions.

Bullying

Children can be exposed to bullying—as victims, perpetrators, bystanders or upstanders. Upstanders, also known as supportive bystanders, attempt to help the victim of bullying in some way by, for example, taking action to stop the bullying or supporting the victim after an incident.

Bullying refers to any intentional and repeated behaviour which causes physical, emotional or social harm to a person who has, or is perceived to have, less power than the person who bullies.

Bullying can have substantial impacts on victims, perpetrators and witnesses, as well as on the broader society. Bullying can happen:
- anywhere (such as at school, at home or in the neighbourhood)
- in person or online
- in an obvious or hidden manner.

Proportion of children aged 12–13 who experienced bullying-like behaviour in the 12 months before the survey, 25 February 2022 (Note the graph is divided roughly into thirds.)

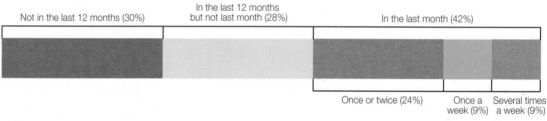

Not in the last 12 months (30%)   In the last 12 months but not last month (28%)   In the last month (42%)

Once or twice (24%)   Once a week (9%)   Several times a week (9%)

Adapted from https://www.aihw.gov.au/reports/children-youth/australias-children/contents/justice-and-safety/bullying

For questions **1–6**, choose the option (**A**, **B**, **C** or **D**) which you think best answers the question.

1 The following dictionary definition refers to which person from the text?

a person who carries out a harmful, illegal or immoral act

A a victim
B a perpetrator
C a bystander
D an upstander

2 Which of the statements are correct according to the graph?

A In the last 12 months, most 12–13-year-old children experienced little bullying.
B In the last 12 months, older children experienced more bullying than younger children in the 12–13-year-old age group.
C In the last 12 months, 24% of the 12–13-year-old children experienced bullying once a week.
D In the last 12 months, 12–13-year-old children experienced bullying 42 times.

3 What is a synonym for 'perceived' as used in the text?

A known   B expected
C considered   D discovered

4 In the last month, what percentage of 12–13-year-old children experienced a form of bullying up to twice a week?

A 9%   B 24%   C 28%   D 30%

5 Which word does **not** go with the other three?

A onlooker   B eyewitness
C bystander   D accomplice

6 The group of 12–13-year-old children which is most represented on the graph includes those who have experienced

A some incidental bullying in the past 12 months.
B no bullying in the past month.
C bullying once or twice a week.
D several weekly bullying incidents.

Read the poem below by RC Scriven then answer the questions.

The Marrog

My desk's at the back of the class
And nobody knows
I'm a marrog from Mars
With a body of brass
And seventeen fingers and toes.
Wouldn't they shriek if they knew
I've three eyes at the back of my head
And my hair is bright purple
My nose is deep blue
And my teeth are half yellow half red?
My five arms are silver with knives on
                 them sharper than spears.

I could go back right now if I like—
And return in a million light years.
I could gobble them all
For I'm seven foot tall
And I'm breathing green flames from my ears.
Wouldn't they yell if they knew
If they guessed that a marrog was here?
Ha-ha they haven't a clue—
Or wouldn't they tremble with fear!
Look, look, a Marrog
They'd all scream—and SMACK.
The blackboard would fall and the
                 ceiling would crack
And the teacher would faint I suppose.
But I grin to myself sitting right at the back
And Nobody nobody knows.

From *I Like This Poem*, Puffin Books, 1979

For questions **1–7**, choose the option (**A**, **B**, **C** or **D**) which you think best answers the question.

1 The narrator of the poem is feeling
  A lazy.   **B** bored.
  C angry.   **D** dangerous.

2 The phrase 'they haven't a clue' is meant to show that the students
  A are too frightened to escape.
  B do not know about the marrog.
  C cannot understand their work.
  D have not been taught anything.

3 The marrog is really a creature
  A from Mars.
  B lost on Earth.
  C in the classroom.
  D of the imagination.

4 It is most likely the teacher is
  A going about her work normally.
  B worried about the ceiling.
  C about to be gobbled up.
  D another alien.

5 From the poem it seems most likely the narrator dislikes
  A teachers.
  B space travel.
  C school work.
  D the other students.

6 The narrator has a desk at the back of the class which lets him
  A sleep.
  B work hard.
  C daydream.
  D annoy students.

7 The narrator believes that if the students turned and looked at him they would
  A faint.
  B be screamed at.
  C tremble with fear.
  D see he had three eyes.

MINI TEST 6: Narrative

11 min

Read the text below then answer the questions.

Dangerous Redheads

It is the worst thing having to go to a new school where everyone knows one another and all the gangs and groups and friendships have been underway since grade one. I arrived in grade five, straight from the hippie commune that I had lived in since I was born. I'd never been to school before and sitting in desks, in rows, having to put my hand up when I wanted to say something, having to do what the teacher told me and having to wear shoes nearly drove me mad. I felt like a caged tiger, all prowling and scratchy and furious. And somehow Cal understood. The teachers didn't understand though; every day was a battle in which they tried to make me docile and tame and obedient and I tried to assert my right to continue being a sort of embryonic female Tarzan.

Cal was always the mediator. He hated conflict but I didn't mind it so much because it gave me a buzz. He'd try to protect me from the teachers—and from myself—and usually he finished up as Pig-in-the-Middle copping flak from both sides.

Even when I got a gang of other kids who could climb trees, throw rocks and create havoc nearly as well as I could, Cal still hung in there.

By Louise Elliott, UQP, 1994

For questions **1–8**, choose the option (**A**, **B**, **C** or **D**) which you think best answers the question.

1 The narrator found the new school difficult because
  A she was a girl.
  B she didn't have a gang.
  C school rules were new to her.
  D Cal was always hanging around.

2 The narrator is
  A an undisciplined person.
  B a primitive person.
  C a savage person.
  D a quiet person.

3 The phrase 'Cal was always the mediator' is meant to show that Cal
  A meddled in other people's affairs.
  B helped solve disputes.
  C played games.
  D was a coward.

4 The narrator was most annoyed by
  A Cal.   **B** her shoes.
  C the students.   **D** copping flak.

5 Conflict in the class made the narrator feel
  A angry.
  B excited.
  C unwanted.
  D distressed.

6 A satisfactory title for the article would be
  A Joining a Gang.
  B Climbing Trees.
  C Beginning School.
  D Pig-in-the-Middle.

7 The word 'docile' is closest in meaning to
  A gentle.   **B** dreary.
  C contented.   **D** manageable.

8 From information in the extract it is most likely that the narrator is
  A hard-working in class.
  B always needing help.
  C athletic and resourceful.
  D quiet and avoids disputes.

MINI TEST 7: Poetry

Read the poem below by Robert Clark then answer the questions.

The Dogman

The dogman dangles from the clouds,
Astride a beam of swinging air
Unrealised hero of the crowds
Whose upturned faces dimly stare.
Like daisies watching from the ground.
Arrayed in far-off random files
Their homage rises without sound
In grave content or drifting smiles.
The earth is open to his eyes
Spread before him like a chart
To the blue-washed blind of sea and sky
To where the mountains lie apart.

From *Exploring Poetry* by James Peek, AH & AW Reed, 1968

For questions **1–7**, choose the option (**A**, **B**, **C** or **D**) which you think best answers the question.

1 A dogman is a
  A dog catcher.
  B parachutist.
  C emergency rescuer.
  D construction worker.

2 The people watching the dogman are
  A laughing.   B clapping.
  C talking.   D silent.

3 The dogman has a clear picture of the scene because he is
  A in the clouds.
  B on a mountain.
  C looking at a chart.
  D working on a tall building.

4 The crowd's attitude towards the dogman is one of
  A fear.
  B respect.
  C concern.
  D amusement.

5 In the poem the word '[a]rrayed' is closest in meaning to
  A strewn.
  B trapped.
  C spread out.
  D in neat rows.

6 The people in the crowd are still smiling because they
  A are standing in daisies.
  B respect the dogman's courage.
  C expect something exciting to happen.
  D are enjoying the show he is giving them.

7 The 'beam' is most likely
  A a sunbeam.
  B swinging air.
  C a steel girder.
  D a rescue platform.

Read the text below then answer the questions.

Kangaroo meat?

Kangaroos are everywhere! There is an estimated 50 million kangaroos in Australia.

They are of significant cultural and spiritual significance for many First Nations Australians and have become an emblem of Australia, appearing on the national coat of arms and in many state and city coats of arms.

A kangaroo appears as the QANTAS logo and the names of sport teams. The national rugby league team is nicknamed the Kangaroos, the national rugby union team is called the Wallabies and the Australian men's soccer team goes by the name the Socceroos. The boxing kangaroo became an Australian sporting symbol in 1983 when it was used in the successful America's Cup yacht challenge.

Roos are unique to this country but some people argue they're badly mismanaged: slaughtered on farms with little regard to animal welfare, hit by cars or exploding in numbers during wet years followed by millions dying of starvation in dry years. One minute they're being culled, the next minute protected.

Regardless of the environmental and health benefits of kangaroo meat, Australians are understandably queasy about the idea of eating them. The main reason why Australians are wary to jump on the kangaroo meat train, however, is more psychological. The animal is widely revered as a symbol of Australia. Kangaroo and kangaroo-related marsupials like wallabies are considered cute and cuddly.

There are people, however, who believe we should eat kangaroo meat, as this would help the kangaroo in the long run. They are a source of low-polluting, native red meat. The commercial kangaroo farming industry exists but it's a very controversial topic.

Roo harvesting divides Australians but there's evidence that a regulated meat industry could be the best thing for ensuring a sustainable kangaroo population.

Even critics of the industry agree the current state of kangaroo management needs to change. It's a shameful situation which appears to be getting worse.

Could eating more kangaroo meat be the key to managing the national animal?

Adapted from https://www.portpirierecorder.com.au/story/7549219/should-we-eat-our-national-animal/

MINI TEST 8

For questions **1–8**, choose the option (**A**, **B**, **C** or **D**) which you think best answers the question.

1 Discussions about the importance of kangaroos could be described as

A a temporary issue.

B an emotive issue.

C a trite issue.

D a settled issue.

2 The main purpose of the text is to

A encourage people to eat kangaroo meat rather than other red meats.

B persuade people of the need to protect kangaroos.

C explain the importance of a balanced attitude to kangaroos.

D prevent drivers from injuring kangaroos on the roads.

3 The title of the text has a question mark. This is to

A raise a complex issue with readers that should be considered.

B encourage readers to reject the eating of kangaroo meat.

C forewarn the reader that the topic may cause distress.

D inform the reader that kangaroos have a population problem.

4 As used in the text, what is a suitable explanation of the word 'culled'?

A the removal of all injured and starving kangaroos

B the choosing of injured and starving kangaroos for transport to a butcher

C the selective slaughter of kangaroos

D the elimination of kangaroos in extreme climatic condition

5 Which sport was this emblem used for?

A boxing

B rugby league

C soccer

D yachting

6 Many Australians won't eat kangaroo meat because

A it has less nutritional value than other red meats.

B kangaroo populations are dwindling.

C of the cruel ways kangaroos are treated.

D they regard kangaroos as being cuddly creatures.

7 Which pair of words from the text has opposite connotations?

A protected—slaughtered

B logo—symbol

C cultural—spiritual

D health—welfare

8 What point from the text does the photograph support?

A Kangaroos are popular as cuddly pets.

B Kangaroos are in abundance in Australia.

C Kangaroos are a source of low-polluting, native red meat.

D Kangaroos are unique to Australia.

MINI TEST 9: Information report

Read the text below then answer the questions.

Yolla

Yolla is the Aboriginal name for a seabird which makes a unique migratory journey each year between Tasmania, Alaska and Japan. Every November the yolla return to Tasmania to hatch their young in rookeries bounded by the pure white sands of the isolated Bass Strait islands. Parent birds feed the fledglings with krill scooped from the crystal-blue waters during their spectacular evening flight. To see thousands of yolla wheeling through the cleanest air in the world is one of the most exhilarating experiences you could have.

Harvesting yolla remains an important social and cultural activity for the First Nations peoples of Tasmania, continuing a tradition maintained from time immemorial. The five-week birding season is historically the time when First Nations families from across Tasmania gather together to work, socialise, speak their language, practise their customs and build their vision of the future.

Eighteen million yolla breed in Tasmania annually. The harvest of less than 300 000 birds is controlled by the prudent management of the First Nations community, which has kept the yolla population flourishing for thousands of years.

Yolla is a native food product exclusive to Tasmania. The meat is available skinned, or traditionally plucked and salted.

Source: Tasmanian Aboriginal Centre 1994 promotional flier, 198 Elizabeth St, Hobart, Tasmania 7000

For questions **1–8**, choose the option (**A**, **B**, **C** or **D**) which you think best answers the question.

1 The First Nations people of Tasmania regard the yolla as important because
   A there are three million of them.
   B of their long migratory journey each year.
   C they have rookeries on the Bass Strait islands.
   D harvesting of yolla provides opportunities for cultural activity.

2 The word 'birding' refers to
   A collecting yolla.
   B a cultural meeting.
   C prudent management.
   D flying between islands.

3 The word 'unique' means
   A very long.
   B spectacular.
   C having no equal.
   D outstanding.

4 The Yolla breeding season occurs
   A after the birds migrate to Japan.
   B before November each year.
   C for a five-week period.
   D annually.

5 The young yolla are fed upon
   A krill collected by their parents.
   B food found on the white island sands.
   C the remains of skinned and plucked birds.
   D food provided by First Nations Tasmanians.

6 From the information provided it can be assumed that yolla harvesting
   A is strictly controlled.
   B is too difficult to manage.
   C will last only a few years.
   D has little commercial value.

7 Yolla harvesting is important because it
   A combines social and commercial activities.
   B means First Nations peoples have to speak their own language.
   C provides First Australians with an important food supply.
   D is the only industry for the First Australians living on the Bass Strait islands.

8 According to the information, yolla harvesting
   A occurs in early November.
   B also occurs in Alaska and Japan.
   C wipes out a large proportion of the flock.
   D existed before white settlement in Australia.

MINI TEST 10: Narrative

Read the text below then answer the questions.

The Empty House

I don't know how I'm going to say this next bit. I don't want to. I can't. I will though. My stomach heaves, my throat hurts. My head is going round and round, but I'll say it. I will get it down even if I die writing it.

Madame Weiss was out in the street. Two policemen were pulling her along by the hair to make her go with them. She was weeping. She was calling for help. I saw families coming out of the buildings to watch: my friends, their brothers and sisters. They followed their parents without a word. Silence. Just silence to drown out the noise Madame Weiss was making.

And then I saw Father and Mother, carrying a suitcase, with two policemen, one on each side of them. I saw them raise their heads and look at my window. I saw that they had seen me, and they saw that I had seen them. Madame Bianchotti pressed her hand tighter and tighter against my mouth to muffle any sound I might make. Father and Mother went away with the others, surrounded by policemen. Within ten minutes there wasn't a Jew left in our little neighbourhood except me.

Well that's it. I've said it. Now I can die. Only I don't want to. Mother's eyes turned towards me. I suppose I'll see those eyes, those figures for the rest of my life.

By Claude Gutman, Turon & Chambers, 1991

For questions **1–6**, choose the option (**A**, **B**, **C** or **D**) which you think best answers the question.

1 The narrator felt he was going to die because
  A Madame Bianchotti had her hand tightly over his mouth.
  B of his grief caused by his family's separation.
  C he had a sickness that would result in death.
  D the police were going to capture him.

2 Within ten minutes of the police leaving the neighbourhood
  A it was deserted.
  B there was one Jew left.
  C there were no Jews left.
  D there was only Madame Bianchotti left.

3 When the narrator uses the phrase 'silence to drown out the noise' he is suggesting that
  A the police were acting secretly.
  B someone had their hand over the narrator's mouth.
  C sometimes silence can seem more frightening than sound.
  D the onlookers' silence showed their lack of interest in the situation.

4 Madame Weiss appealed for help from
  A the two policemen.
  B Madame Bianchotti.
  C her brothers and sisters.
  D anyone in the neighbourhood.

5 The most likely reason that no-one helped the Jews was because
  A everyone believed the police were doing the right thing.
  B they didn't like the way Madame Weiss was screaming.
  C they were afraid they might get taken away too.
  D the Jews were being difficult and uncooperative.

6 The narrator's parents departed without saying goodbye because
  A they did not want the police to suspect that they had a child.
  B Madame Bianchotti had kept the family apart.
  C the journey had not been well planned.
  D the police would not allow it.

Read the text below then answer the questions.

Aphanasy

Once upon a time and far away

in old Russia there was a great and rich trading city called Nizhny Novgorod. It sat on the banks of the mighty river Volga, and every year the merchants sent their wooden ships to trade at towns and cities near and far. But, far beyond the farthest city they had reached, lay a land where no-one had ever been. India. The merchants had heard tales of wonder and magic about this faraway land, but they had heard too that it was a land of a thousand gods and demons, and they were a little afraid to sail to such a far and terrible place.

So one day they called together all the townspeople. They gathered in the bazaar and everyone talked and argued until at last old Nikitin, the most daring of the merchants, said, 'I have a son, young Aphanasy, who is bold and cheerful and wise beyond his years. And best of all, he is lucky. Since I am too old to go myself, let us send Aphanasy to India.'

By Lilith Norman, Random House, 1994

For questions **1–7**, choose the option (**A**, **B**, **C** or **D**) which you think best answers the question.

1 The Russian merchants wanted to go to India
  A to see the gods and demons.
  B to hear tales of wonder and magic.
  C to find new towns with which to trade.
  D because the people in Russia argued.

2 The phrase 'wise beyond his years' tells the reader that Aphanasy
  A was a wise old man.
  B knew more than most people his age.
  C would be smarter when he was older.
  D had taken many years to become wise.

3 Nikitin would not go to India because he
  A didn't have a ship.
  B was getting too old.
  C was afraid of demons.
  D didn't know how to get there.

4 The merchants gathered in a 'bazaar', which is a
  A riverside park.   **B** Russian city.
  C wooden ship.   **D** marketplace.

5 The townspeople had a meeting to
  A talk and argue.
  B send their ships off to trade.
  C choose someone to find India.
  D listen to tales of wonder and magic.

6 After the meeting, it is most likely that Aphanasy
  A refused to go to India.
  B argued with his father.
  C sat on the banks of the Volga.
  D prepared to sail for unknown lands.

7 A 'daring' person is one who would
  A argue a lot.
  B do foolish things.
  C go on adventures.
  D be very successful.

MINI TEST 12: Persuasive text

The Bilbies
An Exciting New Musical for Kids

★★★ *Starring* ★★★
Wilby and **Silby Bilby**
Gaza Galah Bettina Bunny
with a special guest appearance by

The Fairy Princess
Performed by **Maria Cauchi**
Original cast member of **The Phantom of the Opera**

Family Fun at affordable prices!
Child $10 ea. Adults $14 ea. Family pass $38
4 people (Max 2 Adults) (No Booking Fee)
Special Discounts for Groups of 10 or more

Opening January 2023

Pilgrim Theatre City
62 Pitt St City (1 Minute walk from Town Hall Station)
2nd to 21st Jan. Tues. to Sun. 10 am & 2.30 pm

Parramatta Town Hall
One Day only. Tues 23rd Jan.
10 am, 11.30 am & 2.30 pm

Bilby Theatrical Productions, PO Box 3072, Putney, NSW 2112
Bookings Ph: (02) 8809 0006 or (02) 8807 6367

For questions **1–8**, choose the option (**A**, **B**, **C** or **D**) which you think best answers the question.

1 Children most likely to enjoy the show, *The Bilbies*, would be about
A 2 years old.
B 5 years old.
C 12 years old.
D 16 years old.

2 A 'cast member' is one of the
A audience. B writers.
C opera. D actors.

3 At Parramatta Town Hall there
A was one performance.
B were two performances.
C were three performances.
D were five performances.

4 At the Pilgrim Theatre there were at least
A two performances.
B 19 performances.
C 21 performances.
D 34 performances.

5 If a group of twelve children went to see *The Bilbies* they would
A have special seats.
B get seats at a cheaper rate.
C be charged at family prices.
D need to make a phone booking.

6 If it was decided to include a snake in the show, a suitable name would be
A Sonia.
B Maria.
C Blackie.
D Dilby.

7 Which of the following statements are true?
A Maria Cauchi has been The Fairy Princess in *The Bilbies* for many years.
B Parramatta Town Hall is one minute from Town Hall Station.
C There is no booking fee for phone bookings to see *The Bilbies*.
D A family of five would have to pay $38 to see *The Bilbies*.

8 A 'guest appearance' is
A only included when the guest is available.
B a brief appearance by a famous person.
C the most important part in the musical.
D a non-speaking part in a stage show.

Read the texts below then answer the questions.

TEXT 1

From *Pirates of Tahiti* by Alan Horsfield

Hawkins had no idea what had happened. It was as if the Bora Bora Café had slipped back in time!

Without warning Benito stood, grabbed Hawkins under the armpit and hauled him firmly to his feet. The wooden chair rattled back but didn't tumble. His wooden leg stumped solidly on the floor. The few scraggy patrons watched with disinterest. They had seen it all before.

Hawkins was manhandled through the doorway and into the near-deserted street. The multicoloured strip curtain had gone. The brightness of the sun made Hawkins squint as he desperately tried to get his bearings. Everything had changed.

Just outside the doorway the three Chinese labourers were waiting with their baskets on either ends of their shoulder poles.

'Let me go!' begged Hawkins but the grip on his shoulder only got tighter, more claw-like.

'Ow!' groaned Hawkins angrily, hunching his shoulder.

'Easy on the lad,' warned José. Firm but friendly.

Pressure from the bony claw-like grip slackened and Hawkins was able to roll his shoulders a little.

The group made their hurried way towards a collection of small rowing boats rocking at the end of a rickety wharf, a reflective Sparrow at the rear.

A brig of war was majestically anchored a hundred yards away in the Tahitian harbour. It dominated its watery surroundings as if posing for a photo. The lord of the seas—flying a pirate flag!

Irrationally, Hawkins momentarily thought it would make a good photo—if he had his phone!

That brought on a pang of hopelessness. He scrunched up his eyes.

The locals took little interest in the altercations of the strangers as they passed by, though a couple stared as Benito clumped his wooden leg along the timbers. They would be glad when all undesirable visitors left their island.

Hawkins glanced at the group straggling behind. The Chinese labourers were following. And a couple of grubby layabouts, who looked drunk, and a half-naked black man who had merged into the group behind José, with Sparrow dropping to the back.

José growled an order to the ragged contingent, who shuffled awkwardly towards separate rowing boats.

'More landlubbers than seamen!' sniffed Benito as he, José and Hawkins settled into a boat and cast off. 'Cap'n Goode may even make deckhands out of some of them. May? Chinese are good in the galley! Most of 'em can cook!'

To board the *Araucano* they had to climb a rope ladder that hung loosely over the side. José led the way, somehow managing to use his hand-hook to roughly drag the trembling Hawkins up with him. The ladder swung left and right, back and forth, in unpredictable arcs. Hawkins clung on so tightly his knuckles were white.

TEXT 2

From *Rats of Wolfe Island* by Alan Horsfield

I met Rex King on my first visit to the main island. I had only just started at uni and was making the most of my first mid-semester break. I should have been at home catching up on a science assignment, but I was prepared to bluff my way through it—or at least, get an extension of time to 'finish' it. I wasn't about to give up my holiday. I was off to wander around the Pacific—as cheaply as possible, much to my parents' chagrin.

I had just gone into a small wharf-side café looking for something cheap and local to eat. The place was more or less empty. Rex was sitting in a far corner obviously enjoying a plate of fish and chips. I hardly noticed him, being more taken in by such an impressive café being located in such a small tropical town. It was better than any coffee shop on campus.

While waiting to be served I sat at one of the round tables adjacent to the large glassless windows. The cool, salty breeze drifted across the bay. I shut my eyes and let it massage my hot forehead. As a backpacker one tends to do a lot of walking, often in the tropical heat. The locals seem to know better.

He spoke first. 'Mad dogs and Englishmen.'

'I know. Go out in the midday sun,' I answered, not opening my eyes. 'But I'm more the Australian variety.' Then I added with a broad smile, 'Eddie Haite.'

'Where you heading—Eddie?' he asked after stuffing a few more chips into his mouth.

'Thought I might explore this place—the island more than just the town. I'm actually looking for excuses not to make any serious decisions about uni until I return.'

'Procrastinating. A luxury of youth,' he said with a sigh. Then he added, 'Uni could be better than sleeping on some mosquito-infested beach in the middle of a downpour. And no way of finding a dry bed for at least twelve hours. That's when you'll realise that uni isn't all that bad.'

I shrugged and nodded, but I wasn't convinced. It was a bright sunny day and uni had been left far behind in the suburban smog. Right now uni could have been on the moon!

'It has its moments, I guess.' I rambled on about some of the things I liked.

He seemed interested in what I had to say. I gave my biased opinion of what I thought of unis, lecturers and uni traditions in general.

'Sometimes it's not a bad thing to have time off between school and university. Gives one a chance to grow up,' he mused.

'Dad'd prefer I used it to earn some money!' I countered.

He was amused. 'Ever done any lab work?' He tugged gently at a red scarf he had knotted around his neck.

'Sure. Done a bit of science. Like to try a bit of biology. Thought I might have a go at marine biology later on.'

Rex smiled softly—ruefully.

For questions **1–8**, choose the option (**A**, **B**, **C** or **D**) which you think best answers the question.

1 The incidents recorded in the texts take place in
A Australia.
B England.
C the South Pacific.
D South-East Asia.

2 In Text 2, what does Rex King's smile suggest about his thinking?
A He doubted the narrator's intentions.
B He was pleased the narrator had ambition.
C He knew the narrator was incapable of such studies.
D He understood the rigours of tropical life better than most.

3 Who is most out of place in his present environment or situation?
A Captain Goode in Text 1
B Hawkins in Text 1
C Rex King in Text 2
D the narrator in Text 2

4 In Text 1, why is Hawkins's thought about using his phone referred to as being irrational?
A The harbour in Tahiti does not have mobile phone coverage.
B There was no time to take a photo.
C His captors would not permit such a diversion.
D It is a foolish thought considering his dire situation.

5 Which of the following is an example of a metaphor?
A the bony claw-like grip slackened
B Benito clumped his wooden leg along the timbers
C the island more than just the town
D I was prepared to bluff my way through it

6 In Text 2, the relationship between Rex and Eddie is one of
A cautious interplay.
B friendly banter.
C suspicious concern.
D token interest.

7 Which option is characteristic of both characters' behaviour?

	Rex King	Hawkins
A	prying	arrogant
B	trusting	intrepid
C	confident	shocked
D	tentative	indignant

8 The last paragraph of Text 1 suggests that Hawkins's plight will
A persist relentlessly.
B soon improve.
C end unexpectedly.
D continue to worsen.

Read the texts below then answer the questions.

TEXT 1

Largest canyon in the solar system

Mars is famous for its orangey-red hue caused by the iron oxide in its soil. However, the Red Planet's surface, which has been drastically altered by volcanoes, impact craters, crustal movement, and atmospheric conditions such as dust storms, is also home to a wide range of fascinating landform features. High among the list is Valles Marineris—the Solar System's longest and deepest-known canyon.

This massive gorge, which comprises a network of interconnected troughs, extends over 4826 km—a little more than the distance from Perth to Brisbane. It measures 322 km at its widest and 7 km at its deepest. In comparison, the Earth's Grand Canyon spans a 'mere' 445 km long, 28 km wide and about 1.6 km deep!

The canyon's existence was first revealed by NASA's Mariner 9 Spacecraft in 1972. Since then, the camera aboard NASA's Mars Reconnaissance Orbiter—launched to study the Red Planet's geology and climate in 2005—has captured several close-up images of Valles Marineris. However, despite the detailed breathtaking photos, scientists are still unsure how the gigantic chasm formed on the Martian surface.

While the mighty Colorado River carved up the Grand Canyon, the Red Planet was too hot and arid to have a river powerful enough to slash such an enormous abyss across its surface. Therefore scientists believe that Valles Marineris may be the result of volcanic eruptions from the Tharsis region—a vast volcanic plateau in the western hemisphere of Mars.

As the Tharsis region bulge swelled with magma during the planet's first billion years, the surrounding crust was stretched, ripping apart and eventually collapsing into the gigantic troughs of Valles Marineris.

The experts suspect that landslides and ancient rivers may also have played a role in sculpting the canyon into the planet's rusty-red surface.

It is not the Red Planet's only interesting landform feature. Mars is also home to the Solar System's largest volcano. The Olympus Mons on Mars is the tallest-known volcano-topped mountain in the Solar System. Standing an impressive 22 km tall, it is about 2.5 times the height of Mt Everest and has a diameter of 624 km—approximately the same size as the state of Victoria. Although most of the volcano formed over billions of years, some areas are just a few million years old, leading scientists to suspect Olympus Mons is active with the potential to erupt.

Source: https://www.dogonews.com/2021/1/26/the-solar-systems-largest-known-canyon-is-stunning

TEXT 2

What is a meteor shower?

If it's time for a meteor shower, you won't need a telescope, binoculars or a tall mountain to have a 'star gazing' party. You might need a warm sleeping bag and an alarm clock to wake you in the middle of the night. But then just lying down in your own backyard will put you in the perfect spot to enjoy a great show.

A meteor is a space rock—or meteoroid—that enters Earth's atmosphere. As the space rock falls toward Earth, the resistance—or drag—of the air on the rock makes it extremely hot. What we see is a 'shooting star'. That bright streak is not actually the rock, but rather the glowing hot air as the hot rock zips through the atmosphere.

When Earth encounters many meteoroids at once, we call it a meteor shower.

Why would Earth encounter many meteoroids at once? Well, comets, like Earth and the other planets, also orbit the sun. Unlike the nearly circular orbits of the planets, the orbits of comets are usually quite lopsided.

As a comet gets closer to the sun, some of its icy surface boils off, releasing lots of particles of dust and rock. This comet debris gets strewn out along the comet's path, especially in the inner solar system (where we live) as the sun's heat boils off more and more ice and debris. Then, several times each year as Earth makes its journey around the sun, its orbit crosses the orbit of a comet, which means Earth smacks into a bunch of comet debris.

But not to worry! The meteoroids are usually small, from dust particle to boulder size. They are almost always small enough to quickly burn up in our atmosphere, so there's little chance any of them will strike Earth's surface. But there is a good chance that you can see a beautiful shooting star show in the middle of the night!

In the case of a meteor shower, the glowing streaks may appear anywhere in the sky, but their 'tails' all seem to point back to the same spot in the sky. That's because all the meteors are coming at us at the same angle, and as they get closer to Earth the effect of perspective makes them seem to get further apart. It's like standing in the middle of railroad tracks and seeing how the two tracks come together in the distance.

Meteor showers are named for the constellation where the meteors appear to be coming from. So, for example, the Orionids Meteor Shower, which occurs in October each year, appears to be originating near the constellation Orion the Hunter. Some years are better than others for numbers of meteors per hour. Keep in mind: If the moon is full or near full, you may not see many meteors.

Adapted from https://spaceplace.nasa.gov/meteor-shower/en/

MINI TEST 14

For questions **1–8**, choose the option (**A**, **B**, **C** or **D**) which you think best answers the question.

1 Which text topic(s) would be of more interest to geologists?

A Text 1

B Text 2

C Both

D Neither

2 Which solar phenomenon is a person most likely to see with the naked eye?

A Valles Marineris

B Orionids Meteor Shower

C neither the Orionids Meteor Shower nor Valles Marineris

D both the Orionids Meteor Shower and Valles Marineris

3 The word 'mere' in Text 1 is being used in

A a mocking way.

B a scornful way.

C a profound way.

D an ironic way.

4 The writer's intent in Text 2 is to

A engage and alert.

B predict and forewarn.

C inform and reassure.

D educate and recommend.

5 Both texts describe events that are

A enduring.

B repetitive.

C catastrophic.

D unique.

6 In Text 2, when is the best time to go 'star gazing' for a meteor shower?

A any month after October each year

B whenever there is a full moon

C on occasions when meteors appear to come from the Hunter Constellation

D during eruptions on Mars in the Tharsis region

7 How many planets are mentioned by name in the texts?

A one

B two

C four

D five

8 In Text 2, which option is most characteristic of a comet?

A tiny space dust particles

B matter from volcanic eruptions on Mars

C an orbiting object similar to a miniature planet

D an icy ball of rocks and dust

Read the texts below then answer the questions.

TEXT 1

Growing potatoes

When I told a friend I was writing an article about how to grow potatoes he said, 'What's to tell? You throw 'em in a bucket, pile on the soil while they grow, and wait until you have spuds (potatoes)'.

I objected to this suggestion but then I realised he's right. Potatoes are almost as easy to grow as radishes. But there *is* more to growing potatoes.

But why go through the effort if it's easier to buy them at the grocery store? Good question. Like everything else that's grown from home, fresh and homegrown spuds are as close to heaven as you're going to get in this lifetime. And like most everything else in life, a good understanding of where something comes from adds to its appreciation.

Spuds are easy to grow but the wise gardener will benefit from some forethought and preparation. Like most vegetables, potatoes benefit from plenty of sunlight but they also benefit from a cold and harsh winter to kill off pests and parasites.

They need about 20 mL of water per week. Deep, night-time soaking is far superior to daytime surface watering. Ultimately a consistently moist soil is vital to good crop health and production. They prefer soil that is in a well-drained bed.

Try to get those spuds into the ground as early as you can, as soon as the soil is workable. They can handle a bit of frost so capitalise on that and plop them in when you've got an itch of spring fever.

I'll plant potatoes within a week or two of the last frost-free day. Before or after doesn't seem to matter. The plants get busy underneath the soil and won't show their heads until they're ready to. It gives them a chance to harden off ahead of time.

In areas that have long and cold winters, the gardener will want to plant in early or mid-spring for a midsummer harvest. In areas with a milder winter, an additional midsummer crop can be planted.

Most spuds bought in grocery stores are unsuitable for seeding homegrown potatoes. It is safest to purchase seed potatoes.

Plant spuds that are golf-ball size. Some varieties are sold this size while others are much larger. If they are big just cut them into smaller pieces and let them sit overnight. They will develop a protective layer over the cut area which will minimise infection. Ensure that each piece you cut has at least two eyes. Plant these pieces so that the eyes are facing upwards.

Add a 3 mL layer of compost along the sowing trench. Add the potatoes and cover with 10 mL of soil. Wait until they start to grow before doing anything else. They'll rocket up before your eyes!

Adapted from https://gardenerspath.com/plants/vegetables/gimme-those-potatoes-a-spud-growing-guide/

TEXT 2

Growing mushrooms

Mushrooms are notoriously unreliable to grow, partly due to the mass-produced low-quality growing kits that people buy. Almost mystical organisms, they seem to pop up in the wild in an unpredictable way, often only appearing for just a few days before vanishing, not to be seen in the same spot for another year. Yet it is possible to successfully grow gourmet mushrooms at home. How can one have success at home?

Mushrooms on straw

First understand the life cycle of a fungus. Similar to the fruits produced by a tree, mushrooms are the reproductive fruits of a dense, root-like network of cells, called 'mycelium'. In the wild, this white network of fine threads grows out in all directions, breaking down its food into simpler molecules to further fuel its growth. When it runs out of food, it switches into survival mode and produces mushrooms in order to release its spores to the wind and find a better place to live. Fortunately it's possible to recreate and manage this life cycle, and get a fine crop of table mushrooms.

Growing your own mushrooms is definitely more difficult than growing most other crops. Mushroom farming relies on costly sterilisation and climatic control equipment.

Start by growing oyster mushrooms, the easiest variety for any home cultivator. The most common materials to grow oysters on are usually freshly cut hardwood logs or shredded straw. Growing mushrooms on logs can be quite difficult. Growing on straw requires you to sterilise the straw first, to kill off micro-organisms that will compete with your mycelium.

Now the coffee grounds! The beauty of growing mushrooms on fresh coffee waste is that it is already sterilised by the coffee brewing process. Plus, coffee grounds are packed full of nutrients which mushrooms love.

First, order in your spawn. You'll have greater success if you use a high spawn-to-coffee grounds ratio. Use 500 g of oyster mushroom spawn to each 2.5 kg of spent grounds.

Wash your hands and mix your spawn into the bowl, breaking it up and distributing it evenly throughout the coffee grounds. Load the mixture into your cultivation bag or container and close it up tight, ensuring you have cut four air holes.

Place your mushroom bag/container in a warm (18–25 °C) and dark place.

During the next three weeks the spawn will grow across the coffee grounds, turning the whole mixture white as it colonises the mixture. Spray this area twice daily with water. Mushrooms love damp, humid conditions.

Later, tiny little mushrooms burst into life. They will increase in size every day and soon be ready for harvesting—and cooking!

Adapted from 'Growing Gourmet Mushrooms at Home from Waste Coffee' by Adam Sayner, www.growveg.com

For questions **1–8**, choose the option (**A**, **B**, **C** or **D**) which you think best answers the question.

1 The conditions mentioned in each text are the
   A times required before harvesting each crop.
   B amount of space required for a crop.
   C best ways to grow the crops.
   D garden spaces required for each crop.

2 In Text 1, the requirements for growing great potatoes should include
   A soil that drains away water at a steady rate.
   B ground that has been sterilised with coffee waste.
   C a twice daytime spraying of foliage with water.
   D planting when the frosty weather has passed.

3 Which set of instructions warns the gardener to expect crop-growing difficulties?
   A Text 1
   B Text 2
   C Neither
   D Both

4 Which set of instructions gives information on ground microorganism control?
   A Text 1
   B Text 2
   C Neither
   D Both

5 The writer of Text 2 is most critical of
   A mass-produced mushroom-growing kits.
   B the failure to use coffee grounds for nutrients.
   C lack of instruction on how to control growing temperature.
   D mushrooms that are slow growing.

6 In Text 1, when growing potatoes a friend advises 'You throw 'em in a bucket, pile on the soil'.
   This suggests the friend's attitude to growing potatoes is
   A scientific.
   B indifferent.
   C nonchalant.
   D careless.

7 Which of these statements is correct?
   A Growing mushrooms is easier than growing radishes.
   B The best place to get seed potatoes is from the greengrocer.
   C The bigger the potato seed, the better the potato crop.
   D Mushrooms prefer to be grown in a dark indoor area.

8 In Text 1, the term 'their heads' refers to the heads of the
   A mushroom growers.
   B potato plants.
   C people who sell coffee.
   D grocers.

Read the texts below then answer the questions.

TEXT 1

From *The Green Ambulance Caper* by Alan Horsfield

Dusty had a few more questions then sent the burly tree-lopper glumly on his way, with orders to clean up the mess asap!

'Let's go!' Dusty said without explanation, nodding to the van, and we scurried around to get into our front seat.

We made our way to a darker, drearier part of town. Every time Bindi tried to ask Dusty a question he didn't answer. He was lost in thought.

We passed through the suburbs of Brokenwood Glen, Black Forest and finally Scrublands. The streets looked more desolate and deserted but I'm sure there were people in the houses behind their drawn curtains. Some had grey smoke snaking out of black-rimmed chimneys.

I started to feel depressed and wary. Bindi just stared straight ahead.

Finally we turned into Deadwood Lane. The houses were further apart and the vacant blocks were full of scattered yellowing weeds and stunted trees.

Suddenly the road ended as we came up to a huge arched gate with black metal bars.

In the middle of the arch, high above the gate was a sign on a grey marble plaque: **Nettle and Thistledown Mansion**. We were at the Topiary Twins' Mansion. But on the outside.

Dusty rubbed his chin then smiled.

Getting out of the van, he hurried to the security intercom. I heard him say, 'Pizza delivery for the Topiary Twins'. He turned and smiled at us. His clenched fists were held in front of his chest.

We waited. The gates didn't open.

Dusty tried again this time. 'Pizza delivery for the Topiary Twins. Get it while it's hot!'

The gates hummed open.

Dusty jumped into the driver's seat and we roared through before the Topiary Twins realised they had been tricked.

Inside the gates was another world. It was like driving through a well-kept park.

'Just look at that!' muttered Dusty.

'It's terrible,' agreed Bindi.

I felt like asking 'What?' but held my tongue.

'Look at that one,' exclaimed Bindi excitedly, pointing at a privet bush trimmed into the shape of an aeroplane. 'Yuk!'

'So cruel,' murmured Dusty. 'Imagine how the plant feels made to look like a plane?' I could feel his disgust.

'And that one and that one!' Bindi was pointing wildly all over the place. I saw shrubs in the shapes of the Eiffel Tower, an elephant, the Opera House, the Harbour Bridge, a birthday cake and the Queen.

We rounded a wide bend and both Dusty and Bindi gasped.

From *The Green Ambulance Caper* by Alan Horsfield, Hand in Hand Woodslane Press, 2014

TEXT 2

From *The Night of the Scarecrow* by Alan Horsfield

I was getting used to possums on the roof and the creaking of the iron as the roof cooled down during the night when I was in bed. I was getting used to *some* of the other noises.

The shadows in my new room were becoming familiar.

I began dreaming I was running through fields of dead, black birds and being chased by others swooping out of the sky making an 'awking' sound. All the time the scarecrow sat on his hill laughing at my plight.

The harder I tried to escape, the faster I tried to run, the more I seemed to be stuck in the one spot. The birds got closer and closer as they swooped by.

I slowly woke up, not sure where my dream ended and my wakefulness began. At first I wasn't sure if I could still hear the black birds crying out or if it was in my imagination. To my dismay when I strained to hear the sound I could actually hear something like the 'awking' sound. I wasn't sure when I first heard it but after a while I knew it was somewhere out there in the distant dark. And I knew I was awake.

I lay perfectly still, listening. Every so often I would hear a lonesome 'awk'. I couldn't tell if it was getting closer or further away. I wished it would go away. My dream was still fresh in my memory.

I was startled when I heard what I thought was tapping on my window.

Tap. Tap-tap. Tap.

I lay perfectly still, hardly game to turn my head to the window.

The window was just a grey-black hole in a blacker room.

I watched and waited.

When I heard it a second time I went rigid.

Tap. Tap-tap. Tap.

It wasn't my imagination. I definitely heard tapping sounds.

There was nothing for what seemed like half an hour then *Tap. Tap-tap. Tap.*

I was terrified. I lay perfectly still, my body stiff, not daring to call Mum and Dad.

I promised myself not to go to sleep. I didn't want to die in my bed.

But some time later I had fallen into a restless sleep.

When I awoke the next morning the room was bright—full of light. I realised my fear of tapping noises was really more imagination than anything else—until I went out for breakfast.

Jenny was saying to Dad as I came to the table, 'Something was tapping on my window in the night'.

Her comment shocked me. Dad sort of looked up from his coffee as if asking for more information.

'Probably some bush insect on the windowpane,' he offered as an explanation.

I thought that might explain Jenny's window but it seemed odd to me that we both heard it. Could it be two insects doing the same thing? My mind said not likely.

From *Night of the Scarecrow* by Alan Horsfield, Macmillan Education (Trekkers), 2005

For questions **1–8**, choose the option (**A**, **B**, **C** or **D**) which you think best answers the question.

1 Both texts have characters that
A spend time caring for plants.
B are involved in developing and stressful situations.
C have little concern for the wellbeing of children.
D are involved in night-time activities.

2 In Text 1, Dusty's actions could be described as
A rash.
B unfocused.
C forceful.
D confused.

3 Which character expresses the most apprehension?
A Jenny
B the narrator of Text 2
C Dusty
D Bindi

4 The narrator of Text 2 finds the night-time sounds
A unnerving.
B reassuring.
C mystifying.
D intriguing.

5 What was the narrator of Text 2's reaction to the sounds he heard during the night?
A He rationalised the sounds as natural noises.
B He asked his father what caused the sounds.
C He lay perfectly still in his bed so as not to attract attention.
D He went to sleep as quickly as possible.

6 Which words from Text 1 indicate a sense of expected success?
A Dusty rubbed his chin then smiled.
B Bindi just stared straight ahead.
C It was like driving through a well-kept park.
D His clenched fists were held in front of his chest.

7 In Text 1, the suburbs Dusty drives through could best be described as
A cheerless.
B frightful.
C manicured.
D abandoned.

8 In Text 2, where did the narrator initially think the '*Tap. Tap-tap. Tap*' sound came from?
A insects on the windowpane
B possums on the roof
C the creaking of the iron roof
D his dream

Read the texts below then answer the questions.

TEXT 1

The tiny, feathered dinosaur

The recently unveiled Cretaceous-period dinosaur boasts some very unusual features.

When paleontologists discover a new dinosaur species, they usually marvel at the ancient creature's size or speed. However, a new species of a chicken-sized dinosaur is making headlines for a feature rarely associated with the primitive reptiles that dominated the world for over 140 million years—dazzling looks!

The fossil of the exotic, two-legged animal, which roamed Earth about 110 million years ago, was unearthed in north-eastern Brazil in 1995 and exported to Germany later. The dinosaur lay undisturbed among the collections in the State Museum of Natural History until recently, when an inquisitive team of English university researchers decided to take a closer look.

The fossil's location, inside two limestone slabs, helped preserve hidden skeletal elements and soft tissue, allowing the scientists to obtain unprecedented details about the glamorous animal. While the creature's skeleton was similar to that of other small dinosaurs, its exterior was unlike anything discovered before.

The gorgeous dinosaur featured a thick, luxurious mane that most likely could be manipulated to stand on end at will—similar to a peacock's tail. The ancient creature also boasted two tall, ribbon-like structures on either side of its shoulders. The scientists speculate that the 15-cm-long rigid filaments made of keratin—the same protein that makes up human hair and nails—were ornamental and used to attract mates or to intimidate enemies.

'Given its flamboyance, we can imagine the dinosaur may have indulged in elaborate dancing to show off its display structures,' said an investigator.

The researchers believe the fossil was that of a young male dinosaur. 'We cannot prove the specimen is a male but given the disparity between male and female birds, it appears likely the specimen was a male—and young too. This is surprising given most complex display abilities are reserved for mature adult males.'

The dinosaur's fossil was well preserved inside two slabs of stone. In a nod to its origin and looks, the researchers have named the new species *Ubirajara jubatus*. *Ubirajara* means 'lord of the spear' in Brazil's indigenous Tupi language, while *Jubatus* is Latin for 'maned'.

Unfortunately the beautiful dinosaur's existence, which came to light after the findings were published in a journal in 2020, has sparked an uproar in Brazil. The locals believe the scientifically valuable fossil—the first-known non-avian dinosaur—belongs to Brazil and should be returned. However, a paleontologist at the State Museum of Natural History says the fossil's export was sanctioned by Brazilian officials and belongs to the German museum. The researcher told *National Geographic* he is discussing the situation with colleagues in Brazil and believes they will soon reach an amicable solution.

Adapted from https://www.dogonews.com/2021/1/18/tiny-feathered-dinosaur-dressed-to-impress

Carnivorous plants

People often eat plants or parts of plants. Other animals are also plant eaters—grubs, fish and birds. Many animals eat plants at some time. It can be a dangerous world for plants.

It seems strange that a small group of plants eat animals! Not big animals but small insects. Insects are still animals.

These odd little plants often grow in damp, swampy places, where the soil is poor. They add goodness to their diet by eating insects. They don't have teeth but dissolve the insects in special juices, in the same way our stomachs dissolve our food.

How do these plants catch their insects?

The **Venus flytrap** has leaves that are about 1 cm long, with a hinge in the middle. They open like the jaws of an animal. The careless insect crawls over the leaf and brushes against hairs on the leaf. These hairs act like triggers. The two parts of the leaf then snap shut, trapping the insect. The trap stays shut for several days, long enough to turn the soft body of the insect into a liquid that can be absorbed.

Venus flytrap

The trap of the pretty little **sundew** is different. The leaf is about the size of a shirt button. Short, sticky, red hairs grow on the leaf. Tiny drops on the hairs look like small dewdrops. When an insect lands on the leaf, it gets stuck on the hairs. As the insect struggles to escape, other hairs close over it and the plant dissolves the soft parts of the insect. Then the hairs unfold and the winds blow away what is left.

The **pitcher plant** is a vine that grows on trees in tropical forests. Its leaves are about 10 cm long. They are shaped like long vases or tall jugs—or pitchers. Inside the pitcher is sweet-smelling nectar. Curious insects land on top of the pitcher and start crawling down the hairs to the water. The hairs all point down, making it difficult for the insect to return to the top. Suddenly there are no hairs at all and the insect slips into the pool of juice at the bottom of the pitcher to be drowned and dissolved.

pitcher plant

The **bladderwort** floats in marshy ponds. It has no roots, just a few feathery leaves hiding small traps shaped like mini marble bags. Little insects hide in the feathery leaves but when they touch a trapdoor, it opens inwards and the insect swims through—into the trap. The door closes and cannot be pushed open. The small creature becomes plant food.

It can be a dangerous world for insects!

MINI TEST 17

For questions **1–8**, choose the option (**A, B, C** or **D**) which you think best answers the question.

1 The writer of Text 1 states there was 'a nod to its origin'. This implies the paleontologists were

A indifferent to the issue of the name.

B confused about the nature of the dinosaur.

C willing to compromise on scientific findings.

D in agreement about the dinosaur's place in history.

2 In Text 1, what does the word 'flamboyance' suggest about the dinosaur's behaviour?

A It moves like a fire of colourful flames.

B It is floppy and lacks control.

C It attracts attention because of its extravagant actions.

D It is well coordinated and moves with precision.

3 In Text 2, which plant uses a trapdoor-type device to trap its prey?

A the bladderwort

B the pitcher plant

C the Venus flytrap

D the sundew

4 In Text 1, the dispute over the feathered dinosaur relates to

A whether it was male or female.

B who legally owns the fossil.

C what it should be named.

D the purpose of its 15-cm rigid filaments.

5 Which text(s) rely on humour to engage the reader?

A Text 1

B Text 2

C Neither

D Both

6 Carnivorous plants use a variety of methods to get nourishment.
Which two plants hold insects captive for this purpose?

A the bladderwort and the pitcher plant

B the pitcher plant and the sundew

C the Venus flytrap and the bladderwort

D the sundew and the Venus flytrap

7 It can be assumed from Text 1 that the German authorities

A are amenable to the fossil's return to its country of origin.

B will resist all attempts to have the fossil removed from the museum.

C are negotiating with *National Geographic* to dispel any criticism.

D are not convinced the fossil originally belonged to the Brazilians.

8 Carnivorous plants, to convert insects to plant food, must

A crush them.

B dissolve them.

C swallow them.

D dehydrate them.

Read the texts below then answer the questions.

TEXT 1

The origin of *Tiddlywinks*

Tiddlywinks is a game in which small plastic counters are flicked into a central receptacle by being pressed on the edge with a larger counter to make them shoot off like projectiles.

Many people played Tiddlywinks in their childhood but the game is actually taken quite seriously in some parts of the world.

The game began as an adult parlour game in England. A bank clerk had the original patent application in 1888. However, competition was quite fierce and for several years other game publishers came out with their own versions of the game using a variety of names. It became one of the most popular crazes during the 1890s, played by adults and children alike. Throughout the first half of the twentieth century, the adult game's popularity waned.

The strong resurgence of interest in the adult game of Tiddlywinks can be traced back to the inauguration of the Cambridge University Tiddlywinks Club in England in 1955. From that point on, there have always been groups of people who play the game seriously.

Originally Tiddlywinks was a game played on a flat felt mat with sets of small discs called 'winks', a pot, which is the target, and a collection of squidgers, which were larger discs.

Players use a 'squidger' (nowadays made of plastic) to shoot a wink into flight by flicking the squidger across the top of a wink and then firmly pressing it over its edge, propelling the disc into the air.

The offensive objective of the game is to score points by sending your own winks into the pot. The defensive objective of the game is to prevent your opponents from potting their winks.

The game can continue until all winks are potted. The game should be timed, giving 25 minutes to matches between pairs and 20 minutes for singles. A game is over before the time limit when one colour is completely squidged into the pot and the score is settled by potting out. Potting out means the pot is emptied and points are scored based on disc colours. Points are tallied and one point from the losing side is given to the winners.

Tiddlywinks is sometimes considered a simple-minded, frivolous children's game, rather than a strategic adult game. However, the modern competitive adult game of tiddlywinks uses far more complex rules and high-grade equipment. But be sure to use the right words when referring to the pieces. They are fun words, after all, and you may surprise people when you say *winks*, *squidgers* and *tiddlies*.

Adapted from:
https://etwa.org/history/
https://en.wikipedia.org/wiki/Tiddlywinks

TEXT 2

The origin of *Snakes and Ladders*

So you think Snakes and Ladders is a child's board game? If you knew more about it, you might be a little more cautious when you play. Players sliding down snakes were seen as being easily tempted by the evils they encountered during life.

It is based on an ancient Hindu game often used for religious instruction. According to some Hindu sages, good and evil exist in all people, side by side.

In ancient times there was a greater religious aspect to the game. The game actually represented the soul's journey through a series of bodies to nirvana, a form of heaven. Nirvana is the final release from all reincarnations.

Reincarnation refers to the belief that a person's soul will go through a series of bodies, better or worse, according to how that person behaved during a particular life.

At the end of one life, it was believed people were reincarnated to take part in the next life. A good person was rewarded with a better life but a person who was evil could become a lowly, often despised, animal. The journey to perfection would become longer!

The journey is made easier by good deeds. You must climb the ladders and avoid the snakes. This shortens the soul's journey through the series of reincarnations to the state of perfection.

The modern English game is played on much the same board as the ancient boards. It is played with a dice and 'players' are moved along the board according to the number thrown on the dice. It is a bit like an obstacle course where the obstacles are snakes and the ladders are the quick tracks to the winner's square.

In some cultures snakes represent evil. In the game if you do wrong, you slide down the snakes.

In the original game of one hundred squares there were eight ladders and twelve snake's heads. Life has more temptations than rewards!

A person needed to be strong-willed to reach the top square in life without doing or being tempted to do wrong. A player always had the chance of climbing a ladder by being a good person.

A player who slid down a snake revealed the player had been evil. In the square where the tail ended was a picture of a lowly animal, such as a goat, a rat or a donkey, all considered lower forms of life. These were all forms of life an evil person could expect to take after reincarnation.

The squares at the top of each snake's head represent such evils as Disobedience, Pride, Stealing, Lying, Murder, Anger and Greed.

Squares at the foot of the ladders represent such virtues as Faith, Good Conduct, Holiness and Knowledge.

It is now a fun game and no longer seen as a moral journey down the road of life.

Adapted from *Games of the World,* edited by Frederic V Grunfeld, Plenary Publications International, New York, 1975

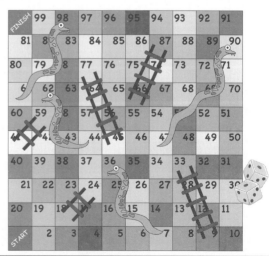

MINI TEST 18

For questions **1–8**, choose the option (**A**, **B**, **C** or **D**) which you think best answers the question.

1 Which game(s) has evolved from a serious adult game to a children's game?

A Tiddlywinks

B Snakes and Ladders

C Both

D Neither

2 Which words are an example of a simile?

A make them shoot off like projectiles

B one of the most popular crazes during the 1890s

C The journey to perfection would become longer!

D Life has more temptations than rewards!

3 In Text 1, what is a 'squidger' in the game of Tiddlywinks?

A another name for a projectile wink

B a disc used to produce momentum in a wink

C a person on the opposing team

D the target pot in which flying discs are collected

4 Which game(s) has ominous overtones?

A Snakes and Ladders

B Tiddlywinks

C Both

D Neither

5 Which is the best description of Tiddlywinks in Text 1?

A It is a game of chance.

B It is a game of expertise.

C It is a game of endurance.

D It is a game of subterfuge.

6 Which statement about the origin of Tiddlywinks and Snakes and Ladders is correct?

A The text only gives the country of origin of Snakes and Ladders.

B The origin of Snakes and Ladders has been lost in antiquity.

C Tiddlywinks and Snakes and Ladders have their origins in England and India respectively.

D Both games had their origin in Cambridge, England.

7 In this phrase from Text 1, what would be a suitable synonym for 'inauguration'?

the inauguration of the Cambridge University Tiddlywinks Club in England

A induction

B establishment

C dedication

D appointment

8 In Text 2, which of these is **not** a penalty in Snakes and Ladders?

A The player was considered evil.

B The player was regarded as having yielded to temptation.

C The player would have a longer journey to perfection.

D The player would miss a go.

Read the texts below then answer the questions.

TEXT 1

From 'Rip Van Winkle' by Washington Irving

Poor Rip was at last reduced almost to despair; and his only alternative, to escape from the labour of the farm and the household clamour of his family, was to take his gun and stroll into the woods. Here he would sometimes seat himself at the foot of a tree and share the contents of his pack with the hungry Wolf, who he saw as a fellow-sufferer.

'Poor Wolf,' he would say, 'the family treats you poorly but don't worry for as long as I'm around you will always have a friend!'

Wolf would wag his tail, look wistfully in his master's face, and if dogs can feel pity I believe he responded with the same sentiment.

In a long ramble on that fine autumn day, Rip had unconsciously scrambled to one of the highest parts of the Catskill Mountains. He was after his favourite sport of hunting, and the still solitudes had echoed and re-echoed with the reports of his gun.

Panting and fatigued, he threw himself, late in the afternoon, on a green knoll, covered with mountain mosses, that crowned the brow of a precipice. From an opening between the trees he could overlook the lower country for many a mile of rich woodland. He saw at a distance the mighty Hudson River, far, far below him, moving on its silent but majestic course, with the reflection of clouds, or the sail of a ship slipping by on its glassy surface.

On the other side he looked into a deep mountain glen, wild and lonely, the bottom filled with fragments from the impending cliffs, and scarcely lit by the reflected rays of the setting sun.

For some time Rip lay musing on this scene; evening was gradually advancing. The mountains began to throw their long blue shadows over the valleys. He saw that it would be dark long before he could reach the village, and he heaved a heavy sigh when he thought of encountering the demanding hassles of family life.

As he was about to descend he heard a voice from a distance hallooing, 'Rip Van Winkle! Rip Van Winkle!'

He looked round but could see nothing but a solitary crow winging its flight across the mountain. He thought his fancy must have deceived him, and turned again to descend, when he heard the same cry in the still evening air.

'Rip Van Winkle! Rip Van Winkle!'—at the same time Wolf bristled up his back, and giving a low growl, skulked to his master's side, looking fearfully down into the glen.

Rip felt a vague apprehension stealing over him; he looked anxiously in the same direction, and saw a strange figure slowly toiling up the rocks and bending under the weight of something he carried on his back.

From *Swiss Family Robinson* by Johann David Wyss

The tempest had raged for six days, and on the seventh seemed to increase. The ship had been so far driven from its course, that no one on board knew where we were. Everyone was exhausted with fatigue and watching. The shattered vessel began to leak in many places, the oaths of the sailors were changed to prayers, and each thought only how to save his own life.

'Children,' I said to my terrified boys, Fritz, Ernest and Jack, who were clinging round me, 'God can save us if he will. To him nothing is impossible; but if he thinks it good to call us to him, we shall not be separated.'

My excellent wife dried her tears, and from that moment became more tranquil. We knelt down to pray for the help of our Heavenly Father; and the fervour and emotion of my innocent boys proved to me that even children can pray and find peace in prayer.

We rose from our knees strengthened to bear the afflictions that hung over us. Suddenly we heard amid the roaring of the waves the cry of 'Land! Land!'

At that moment the ship struck on a rock; the concussion threw us down. We heard a loud cracking, as if the vessel was parting asunder; we felt that we were aground, and heard the captain cry, in a tone of despair, 'We are lost! Launch the boats!'

These words were a dagger to my heart, and the lamentations of my children were louder than ever.

I then recollected myself, and said, 'Courage, my darlings, we are still, above water, and the land is near. God helps those who trust in him. Remain here, and I will endeavour to save us.'

I went on deck, and was instantly thrown down, and wet through by a huge sea; a second followed. I struggled boldly with the waves, and succeeded in keeping myself up, when I saw, with terror, the extent of our wretchedness. The shattered vessel was almost in two; the crew had crowded into the boats, and the last sailor was cutting the rope. I cried out and prayed them to take us with them; but my voice was drowned in the roar of the tempest, nor could they have returned for us through waves that ran mountains high. All hope from their assistance was lost.

But I was consoled by observing that the water did not enter the ship above a certain height. The stern, under which lay the cabin which contained all that was dear to me on earth, was immovably fixed between two rocks.

For questions **1–8**, choose the option (**A**, **B**, **C** or **D**) which you think best answers the question.

1 In Text 2, what saved the ship from sinking during the storm?

A The crew cut the ropes that were securing the ship.

B The tempest become less severe.

C The ship was held fast between two rocks.

D The family managed to keep water out of the ship.

2 In Text 2, which action followed the sailors' change of heart as expressed in the words 'each thought only how to save his own life'?

A They ignored the pleas of the ship's passengers.

B They changed their oaths to prayers.

C They considered their options for saving the ship.

D They made show of intending to return to the ship.

3 Choose the option that is characteristic of each character's behaviour.

	Rip Van Winkle	Father in Text 2
A	proactive	paternal
B	trusting	brave
C	confident	forgiving
D	indolent	protective

4 In Text 1, Wolf reacted to the arrival of the stranger by becoming

A vigilant.

B nonplussed.

C subdued.

D playful.

5 The first paragraph of Text 1 suggests that Rip Van Winkle was

A a dutiful husband.

B a simple malingerer.

C an industrious farmer.

D a successful hunter.

6 The father in Text 2 says the ship 'was parting asunder'.

By this he means it was

A departing for a safer place.

B coming adrift in the storm.

C breaking up in the storm.

D closing all its cargo.

7 In Text 1, who or what was 'looking fearfully down into the glen'?

A Rip himself

B a solitary crow in flight

C a stranger with a load on his back

D Rip's dog, Wolf

8 In which text(s) does a character enjoy spending time in natural surroundings?

A Text 1

B Text 2

C Both

D Neither

Read the texts below then answer the questions.

TEXT 1

Exoplanet Wasp-76b

Scientists have found evidence of rain on an exoplanet. Exoplanets are worlds orbiting other stars and they come in a wide variety of sizes, from gas giants larger than Jupiter to small, rocky planets about as big around as Earth or Mars. They can be hot enough to boil metal or locked in deep freeze. They can orbit their stars so tightly that a 'year' lasts only a few days; they can orbit two suns at once. Some exoplanets are sunless rogues, wandering through the galaxy in permanent darkness. Wasp-76b is what astronomers call an exoplanet. Wasp-76b, which is 640 light years away, is an ultra-hot gas giant.

But don't get too excited about the prospect of life on this world since, instead of water, the rainfall consists of extremely hot vapour droplets of iron. This is because the planet is 'tidally locked' (like the Moon's orbit about Earth) and only ever shows one face, its day side, to its parent star, while its cooler night side remains in perpetual darkness.

On the day side, which is 1000 degrees hotter, molecules separate into atoms and iron evaporates into the atmosphere to form metallic clouds. The extreme temperature difference between the day and night sides produces ferocious winds that carry the iron vapour to the cooler night side, where temperatures decrease to about 1500 °C and the iron condenses and falls as rain that constantly peppers the planet's gas surface and vanishes beneath it.

It could be said that this planet gets rainy in the evening, except it rains iron!

The observations came from a new instrument that was originally designed to hunt for Earth-like planets around sun-like stars. It does this by spotting the dip in starlight that occurs as a planet sails across the face of the star.

For giant planets that are very close to their home star, detecting these transits is an easier task as they block out more light than the more distant planets. Scientists have now moved on to more refined observations to see which gases are present in the planet's atmosphere.

The latest observations go further still and compare the gases present in the leading edge of the planet as it passes across the face of the star and the trailing edge.

For Wasp-76b, this revealed iron vapour at the leading edge, where the prevailing 10,000 km/h wind would be blowing from the day side into the night side. But the signal was absent from the trailing edge, suggesting that all the iron had rained down on the night side by the time the circulating wind came back around.

Adapted from https://www.bbc.com/news/science-environment-51828871

TEXT 2

Dust and life on other planets

It turns out that even in real life, dust is important to worlds outside of Earth! Especially if we are trying to find out if they are habitable. We have learned that dust can cool the hot surface and warm the climate of a planet, making it more suitable for life. On the other hand, larger amounts of dust can make it hard to find habitable planets. And actually, if a planet does host life, dust might hide the signs of it!

There are millions of planets outside our solar system; we call them exoplanets. Finding life (or conditions suitable for life) on a different planet is one goal for many space missions. By 'suitable' we mean the planet is warm enough to have liquid water on its surface. After all, water is absolutely vital for life on Earth.

Planets get their warmth from the star they orbit. On Earth, we get our warmth from the sun—a yellow dwarf star. But most stars in our galaxy are red dwarfs, which are much smaller and cooler than our sun. The only chance for a planet orbiting a red dwarf to be warm and suitable for life (or habitable) is for it to be very close to the star. But then gravity 'locks' the planet to that star—it always has the same side facing it. They have a warm day side and a dark side which can get pretty cold.

This is where airborne dust can come to the rescue. Dust is found on dry land surfaces that are not solid rock and it can be picked up by winds. So the more dry land there is, the more dust there should be—both on the surface and in the planet's atmosphere. Airborne dust deflects starlight, stopping it from reaching the planet's surface.

This cools down the planet. On the other hand, dust can prevent warmth from the surface escaping into space like the greenhouse effect on Earth.

Our planet Earth has an amazing system! The sun has kept Earth warm enough for billions of years, which has made life possible. But then, living organisms are also helping shape Earth's climate through biochemical feedbacks.

The universe is an enormous place, so chances are there are other planets like ours. Imagine how wonderful it would be if dust turned out to be the key to them.

Our results of studies strongly suggest that airborne dust can greatly widen the habitable zone on tidally locked planets—that is, even planets further from the star could support life. Dust first cools the day side, which otherwise can get pretty hot. Second, it warms the dark side, which otherwise could get really cold.

Adapted from https://sciencejournalforkids.org/wp-content/uploads/2020/07/dust_article.pdf

MINI TEST 20

For questions **1–8**, choose the option (**A**, **B**, **C** or **D**) which you think best answers the question.

1 Both texts mention exoplanets. What are exoplanets?

A planets that exist outside our solar system

B planets that only ever show one face to its parent star

C planets where prevailing winds blow from the day side to the night side

D planets that are huge and very close to their home star

2 What makes Exoplanet Wasp-76b unusual?

A It is 640 light years from Earth.

B It can orbit two suns at once.

C It wanders the galaxy in permanent darkness.

D It rains molten iron droplets.

3 Which statement about tidally locked planets is correct?

A Tidally locked planets rotate faster around their sun than other planets.

B Tidally locked planets do not have airborne dust particles.

C Tidally locked planets have a hot side and a cold side.

D Tidally locked planets support living organisms through biochemical feedbacks.

4 According to Text 1, the moon is like an exoplanet because it

A has an orbit that is constant.

B only ever shows one face to our solar system's sun.

C never gets sufficient rain to make it habitable.

D has dust that constantly peppers the surface then vanishes without trace.

5 The writers of Texts 1 and 2 were mainly concerned with

A the relative locations of planets in space.

B surface differences of remote planets.

C influences of size on precipitation rates on planets.

D factors affecting the possibility of life on distant planets.

6 In which text(s) do the writers suggest their subject may give an indication of life beyond Earth?

A Text 1

B Text 2

C Both

D Neither

7 How do the writers of both texts feel about something positive coming out of the research?

A professionally cautious

B basically negative

C somewhat sceptical

D supremely enthused

8 According to Text 2, which of the following is **not** a feature of dust?

A It stops starlight from reaching a planet's surface.

B It is found on the surface of solid rock planets.

C It has a cooling effect on the hot surface of a planet.

D It can lead to a warmer climate for a planet.

Read the texts below then answer the questions.

TEXT 1

Abbott and Costello

Abbott and Costello were an American comedy duo whose work in radio, film and television made them the most popular comedy team of the 1940s and early 1950s and the highest-paid entertainers in the world during World War II. Their patter routine 'Who's on first?' is considered one of the best-known comedy routines of all time. Their popularity waned in the early 1950s due to overexposure and changing tastes in comedy, and their film and television contracts lapsed. The partnership ended soon afterwards.

While they had crossed paths earlier a few times, the two comedians first worked together in 1935 doing burlesque (exaggerated comedy) acts in New York City.

They were encouraged to have a permanent pairing. The duo built an act by refining and reworking numerous comic sketches with Abbott as the devious straight man and Costello as the dimwitted comic.

The duo's first known radio broadcast was in 1938. The similarities between their voices made it difficult for radio listeners (as opposed to stage audiences) to tell them apart with their rapid-fire banter. As a result, Costello affected a high-pitched, childish voice. 'Who's on first?' was first performed for a national radio audience shortly after. They performed on the radio as regulars for two years, while also landing roles in a Broadway revue in 1939.

In 1940 Hollywood's Universal Studios signed them for supporting roles in the musical *One Night in the Tropics*. Abbott and Costello stole the picture with several classic routines, including the 'Who's on first?' routine. They were given a two-picture contract. Their second film was a massive hit, earning $4 million at the box office and launching Abbott and Costello as stars.

Then in 1943 Costello was stricken with rheumatic fever and was bedridden for six months.

In 1945 a rift developed when Abbott hired a domestic servant who had been fired by Costello. Costello refused to speak to his partner except when performing. The following year they made two films in which they appeared as separate characters rather than as a team.

Abbott and Costello reunited as a cinema team in 1947 in a sequel to their 1941 hit. This was followed by a series of Hollywood films.

In January 1951, Abbott and Costello joined the roster of rotating hosts of a TV series.

During the 1950s, Abbott and Costello's popularity waned with the emergence of the Dean Martin and Jerry Lewis comedy duo.

In 1966, Abbott voiced his character in a series of 156 five-minute Abbott and Costello cartoons made by Hanna-Barbera. Lou's character was voiced by another actor. Bud Abbott died of cancer in 1974. Costello had died in March 1959 of a heart attack just short of his 53rd birthday.

'Who's on first?' was named by *Time* magazine (1999) as the best comedy routine of the 20th century.

Adapted from https://en.wikipedia.org/wiki/Abbott_and_Costello

Dean Martin and Jerry Lewis

Singer Dean Martin and comedian Jerry Lewis were an American comedy duo. They met in 1945 and debuted on 25 July 1946. As a team they lasted ten years to the day. Before they teamed up, Martin was a nightclub singer while Lewis performed a comedy act lip-synching (miming) to records.

In their first club act they were so badly received they were threatened with contract termination. The duo responded by abandoning pre-scripted gags and instead began improvising. Martin sang and Lewis dressed as a waiter, dropping plates and making a shambles of Martin's songs and a mockery of the club's decorum. They joked and delivered slapstick to great fanfare. Their club success led to well-paying comedy routines in top New York nightclubs.

A radio series, *The Martin and Lewis Show*, ran from 1948–53, winning them spots on live TV variety shows.

In 1949 they debuted a TV version of their radio show, drawing lacklustre reviews. Also that year they were signed by Paramount Pictures as comedy relief for a film.

Although there had been a number of successful film teams before, Martin and Lewis were different. Both were talented entertainers but being good friends on and off stage gave their acts an edge.

They were the hottest act in America during the early '50s and the highest paid act in show business according to a 1951 *Life* magazine article. One of their tours, promoting their latest film, was so successful audiences wouldn't leave their seats. Martin and Lewis began doing 'free shows' afterwards on fire escapes or from dressing-room windows to adoring fans.

However, the pace and the pressure soon took their toll. Martin usually had the thankless job of the straight man and his singing had yet to develop. Critics praised Lewis, and while they admitted Martin was the better partner, most of them claimed Lewis was the real talent of the team.

After five years at Paramount, Martin became tired of scripts limiting him to colourless romantic leads while parts of their films centred on the antics of Lewis. Eventually they could no longer work together, especially when Martin angrily told Lewis that to him he was 'nothing ... but a dollar sign'.

The use of their full names in their popular radio show helped them launch successful solo careers after parting.

In 1989, the two reunited for the last time in Las Vegas. Lewis thanked Martin for the years of joy he gave the world. He joked, 'Why we broke up, I'll never know'.

Martin died on Christmas Day 1995. Lewis, nicknamed the King of Comedy, died in 2017.

Adapted from https://en.wikipedia.org/wiki/Martin_and_Lewis

For questions **1–8**, choose the option (**A**, **B**, **C** or **D**) which you think best answers the question.

1 Both texts mention that during their careers each duo had
  A tours to overseas military bases.   **B** a partner who was too ill to perform.
  C periods when the duo separated.   **D** a personal entertainment success.

2 The comedy duo teams of Abbott and Costello and Martin and Lewis lasted until the death of one member. This statement is true
  A for both duo teams.   **B** for neither pair of entertainers.
  C for Martin and Lewis only.   **D** for Abbott and Costello only.

3 According to Text 2, Costello adopted a high-pitched, childish voice for the duo's radio shows because
  A it made the interaction between the partners more amusing.
  B constant on-air radio sketches put undue stress on Costello's voice.
  C it made a dim-witted contrast with Abbott's natural voice.
  D radio audiences couldn't tell them apart when using their stage voices.

4 Which option is **not** a reason for the demise of the Abbott and Costello radio show?
  A the success of Dean Martin and Jerry Lewis
  B the inability to adapt to a cinema audience
  C the advent of television
  D the failure of the 'Who's on first?' routine

5 The 'straight man' is the person in a comedy duo who speaks lines which give another comedian the opportunity to make jokes.
  Which of the partners was the straight man?
  A both Dean Martin and Bud Abbott   **B** both Jerry Lewis and Lou Costello
  C Dean Martin only   **D** Bud Abbott only

6 Which entertainment role lifted Abbott and Costello into stardom?
  A the 'Who's on first?' routine
  B the box office success of their second film
  C performing burlesque acts in New York City
  D the musical *One Night in the Tropics*

7 Choose the option that shows each entertainer's early career.

	Bud Abbott	**Lou Costello**	**Dean Martin**	**Jerry Lewis**
A	burlesque	burlesque	nightclub singer	lip-synching
B	comedian	stage acts	comedian	radio comic
C	film star	radio comic	film star	slapstick
D	radio shows	TV host	pop singer	TV appearances

8 Which entertainer(s) received the highest accolade for their contribution to comedy?
  A Dean Martin   **B** Bud Abbott
  C Dean Martin and Jerry Lewis jointly   **D** Bud Abbott and Lou Costello jointly

Read the poem below by Henry Kendall then answer the questions.

Bell-birds

1 By channels of coolness the echoes are
   calling,
And down the dim gorges I hear the creek
   falling;
It lives in the mountain, where moss and the
   sedges
Touch with their beauty the banks and the
   ledges;
Through breaks of the cedar and sycamore
   bowers
Struggles the light that is love to the flowers.
And, softer than slumber, and sweeter than
   singing,
The notes of the bell-birds are running and
   ringing.

2 The silver-voiced bell-birds, the darlings of
   day-time,
They sing in September their songs of the
   May-time.
When shadows wax strong and the thunder-
   bolts hurtle,
They hide with their fear in the leaves of
   the myrtle;
When rain and the sunbeams shine mingled
   together
They start up like fairies that follow fair
   weather,
And straightway the hues of their feathers
   unfolden
Are the green and the purple, the blue and
   the golden.

3 October, the maiden of bright yellow tresses,
Loiters for love in these cool wildernesses;
Loiters knee-deep in the grasses to listen,
Where dripping rocks gleam and the leafy
   pools glisten.
Then is the time when the water-moons
   splendid
Break with their gold, and are scattered or
   blended
Over the creeks, till the woodlands have
   warning
Of songs of the bell-bird and wings of the
   morning.

4 Often I sit, looking back to a childhood
Mixt with the sights and the sounds of the
   wildwood,
Longing for power and the sweetness to
   fashion
Lyrics with beats like the heart-beats of
   passion—
Songs interwoven of lights and of laughters
Borrowed from bell-birds in far forest
   rafters;
So I might keep in the city and alleys
The beauty and strength of the deep
   mountain valleys,
Charming to slumber the pain of my losses
With glimpses of creeks and a vision of
   mosses.

For questions **1–6**, choose the option (**A**, **B**, **C** or **D**) which you think best answers the question.

1 In stanza 1, the poet states that 'the echoes are calling'.

What is the poet mostly suggesting?

A The bellbirds are singing in a remote place.

B There is a variety of overpowering sounds in mountains.

C Individual bellbird sounds are difficult to isolate.

D The notes of the bellbirds are ringing in the poet's ears.

2 What does 'it' (line 3) refer to in stanza 1?

A a bellbird environment

B a flowing creek

C sycamore bowers

D struggling sunlight

3 In stanza 3, the poet uses the literary technique of personification.

What is he personifying?

A the month of October

B yellow flowers of the forest

C the knee-deep grasses

D glistening pools of water

4 In stanza 4, what does the poet admit to having a deep yearning for?

A the city and its alleys

B to sit looking back to his childhood

C the sights and sounds of the wildwood

D songs interwoven of lights and laughter

5 Of the four numbered stanzas, which is a personal reflection?

A 1   B 2   C 3   D 4

6 What does 'When shadows wax strong' in stanza 2 suggest is happening?

A The sunbeams have made the shadows less intense.

B The approaching storm is causing shadows to darken.

C The colours are being drained from the bellbirds' plumage.

D The thunderbolts are giving everything an eerie colour.

Read the poem below then answer the questions.

Calligrams are also commonly called shape poems.

Adapted from
https://literacyideas.com/7-types-of-poetry-for-kids/

For questions **1–6**, choose the option (**A**, **B**, **C** or **D**) which you think best answers the question.

1 A suitable title for this calligram would be

A Mug of soup.

B A winter's nightcap.

C Café souvenir.

D Refreshments for the athletic.

2 When in use the contents of the mug would most likely produce a feeling of

A tranquillity and contentment.

B weariness and relief.

C solace and independence.

D tension and foreboding.

3 Which word from the calligram refers to the distinctive taste of the contents of the receptacle?

A vapour

B steam

C warmth

D flavour

4 A mug like the one in the graphic would quite likely be used in a

A restaurant.

B fast-food café.

C takeaway outlet.

D family home.

5 The most likely reason 'aroma' and 'vapour' are above the main graphic is because they are

A the most important feature of a mug.

B features of the mug's contents that rise from hot drinks.

C ways most people remember hot drinks.

D words that create an emotive response in the reader.

6 Most of the words in the calligram relate to the sense of

A taste.

B sight.

C tactility.

D smell.

Read the poem below by David Bateson and answer the questions.

City to Surf

Ten in the morning
a packed city street—
thousands of people
with jogger-clad feet.

A pistol goes bang;
competitors start
the longest tough race
from the city's heart.

Past the green gardens
and up the steep hill,
through the bright tunnel
the runners mill.

Stride after stride
as spectators shout,
onward and onward
the runners stretch out.

Past parks and houses
and sparkling blue bays
now they must feel
they've been running for days.

Up near the lighthouse
on top of the cliff,
still they keep moving
with muscles stiff.

At last there's a glimpse
of the sand on the beach
and the white foaming surf
is just within reach.

Feet may be blistered
yet still the backs bend—
here's the Pavilion;
it's almost the end.

Though the champ gets the trophy
a medallion's fine,
once you cross over
the finishing line ...

Source: *Orbit Magazine*

For questions **1–6**, choose the option (**A**, **B**, **C** or **D**)
which you think best answers the question.

1   The City to Surf race could best be described as
  A strongly contested.
  B challenging.
  C tedious.
  D brutal.

2   As used in the poem, the word 'mill' means
  A advance swiftly in a competitive situation.
  B cheer unnecessarily boisterously.
  C move around in a disorganised fashion.
  D hurry in a specific direction.

3   The course of the race could best be described
  A producing unpredictable challenges.
  B providing impressive views.
  C giving a sense of satisfaction.
  D lacking variety and interest.

4   By the end of the race the runners feel
  A disappointed they did not win.
  B thrilled with their medallions.
  C prepared for the next race.
  D satisfied to have completed the course.

5   A 'pavilion' is a
  A large open building for spectators.
  B temporary medical centre.
  C dressing shed for competitors.
  D place where awards are handed out.

6   What would have been the most pleasant sight
for the runners during the race?
  A the sparkling bays
  B the green gardens
  C the lighthouse
  D the beach

Read the poem below by TS Eliot then answer the questions.

Macavity: the Mystery Cat

Macavity's a Mystery Cat: he's called the Hidden
    Paw—
For he's the master criminal who can defy the Law.
He's the bafflement of Scotland Yard, the Flying
    Squad's despair:
For when they reach the scene of crime—
    Macavity's not there!

Macavity, Macavity, there's no-one like Macavity,
He's broken every human law, he breaks the law
of gravity.
His powers of levitation would make a fakir stare
And when you reach the scene of crime—
    Macavity's not there!
You may seek him in the basement, you may look
    up in the air—
But I tell you once and once again—Macavity's
    not there!

Macavity's a ginger cat, he's very tall and thin;
You would know him if you saw him for his eyes
    are sunken in.
His brow is deeply lined with thought, his head is
    highly domed;
His coat is dusty from neglect, his whiskers are
    uncombed.
He sways his head from side to side with
    movement like a snake;
And when you think he's half asleep, he's always
    wide awake.

Macavity, Macavity there's no-one like Macavity,
For he's a fiend in feline shape, a monster of
    depravity.
You may meet him in the by-street, you may see
    him in the square—
But when a crime's discovered, then Macavity's
    not there!

From *Old Possum's Book of Practical Cats*, Faber & Faber

For questions **1–6**, choose the option
(**A**, **B**, **C** or **D**) which you think best answers
the question.

1 Macavity could best be described as a
    A clumsy thief.
    B practical pet.
    C cunning feline.
    D playful prankster.

2 Macavity's expertise is his ability to
    A adopt a threatening demeanour.
    B pretend to be asleep.
    C hide in the basement.
    D be nowhere near the crime scene.

3 Macavity's owner is most likely to
consider Macavity as
    A an apprehensive cat.
    B a pampered cat.
    C an affectionate cat.
    D an independent cat.

4 Macavity 'breaks the laws of gravity'.
This statement is meant to show how
    A Macavity seems to do the
       impossible.
    B quickly Macavity can escape.
    C easy it is to avoid obeying the law.
    D inefficient the law enforcers are.

5 Macavity's attitude to Scotland Yard
and the Flying Squad could best be
described as
    A fearful.   **B** supercilious.
    C envious.   **D** distrustful.

6 For Scotland Yard and the Flying
Squad, catching Macavity is
    A extremely frustrating.
    B a dangerous task.
    C of little importance.
    D a routine assignment.

Read the poem below by J Pretulsky then answer the questions.

Towering Giant

In a darksome domain
remorseless and cold stands a
towering giant
grotesque to behold.
He hulks like a mountain,
his head in the sky,
and all who approach him
will certainly die.

The towering giant
by stretching his hands
turns trees into sawdust
and rocks into sand.
One stamp of his foot
and the mountaintop shakes
and winds turn to tempests
with each breath he takes.

Should you land in his clutches
he'll grind you to crumbs,
or crush you to powder
beneath his giant thumbs.
The towering giant
a thousand feet tall
will reduce you to nothing
to nothing at all.

From *The Headless Horseman Rides Tonight*, Faber &
Faber, 1980

For questions **1–6**, choose the option (**A, B, C**
or **D**) which you think best answers the question.

1 As described in the poem the towering
giant
A wilfully causes destruction and suffering.
B is a mild creature with a rough
appearance.
C can react violently and unpredictably.
D is a misunderstood monster.

2 Anyone unfortunate enough to meet the
towering giant will be
A whipped off in strong winds.
B crushed into sand.
C turned into sawdust.
D ground down to crumbs.

3 The towering giant lives in a land that
A has long, dark, moonless nights.
B is surrounded by high, harsh mountains.
C has a never-ending, harsh environment.
D is stricken with grief and sorrow.

4 To say you 'land in his [the giant's]
clutches' is another way of saying you are
A abandoned in a remote land.
B powerless to escape his hands.
C imprisoned in a cage.
D not safe from discovery.

5 The giant is described as being 'grotesque
to behold'.
This suggests the giant is
A too large to grasp.
B of gigantic stature.
C repulsive to look at.
D grossly ill-mannered.

6 If the towering giant were to clap his
hands, the result would
A destroy all wildlife.
B reduce the land to rubble.
C cause a violent storm.
D force the moon to go down.

Read the poem below by Fred Briggs then answer the questions.

The Star Tribes

Look, among the boughs. Those stars are men.
There's Ngintu, with his dogs, who guards the
    skins
of Everlasting Water in the sky.
And there's the Crow-man, carrying on his
    back
the wounded Hawk-man. There's the serpent,
    Thurroo,
glistening in the leaves. There's Kapeetah,
the Moon-man, sitting in his mia-mia.*

And there's those Seven Sisters, travelling
across the sky. They make the real cold frost.
You hear them when you're camped out on
    the plains.
They look down from the sky and see your fire
and 'Mai, mai, mai,' they'd sing out as they run
across the sky. And, when you wake, you find
your swag, the camp, the plains, all white with
    frost.

*Traditional shelter of First Nations Australians

Sources:
https://ozpoemaday.wordpress.com/2012/03/23/the-star-
tribes-by-fred-biggs
The Bulletin, 6 July, Vol. 81 no. 4195 960

For questions **1–6**, choose the option (**A**, **B**, **C**
or **D**) which you think best answers the question.

1 What activity is the narrator of the poem
   involved in?
   A hunting for food in the boughs of trees
   B preparing to make camp for the night
   C searching for firewood for his camp
   D reflecting on the spirits the stars
      represent

2 Where was the Moon-man sitting?
   A in his mia-mia
   B by his campfire on the plains
   C among the stars
   D in the boughs of a tree

3 Which of the star men has a dog?
   A Hawk-man
   B Crow-man
   C Ngintu
   D Kapeetah

4 Which statement is most likely correct?
   A The people of the Star Tribes have
      passed on from this world.
   B There is a snake in the grass near the
      campfire.
   C The people of the Star Tribes
      represent a changing First Nations
      Australian culture.
   D Camping on the plains is
      uncomfortable and dangerous.

5 The tone conveyed in the poem is one
   of
   A regret.
   B nostalgia.
   C optimism.
   D uncertainty.

6 What does the narrator expect the
   Seven Sisters to bring?
   A   a peaceful sleep
   B Everlasting Water
   C a frosty morning
   D a campfire

Read the poem below by Elaine Horsfield then answer the questions.

Bosley

Bosley was getting fed up with his home.
The food was an utter disgrace.
They fed him with fish that came out of a tin
Of a quality really just fit for the bin.
And he knew he was getting decidedly thin.
So he set out to find a new place.

He followed his nose till he came to a street
That sent him right into a spin.
For the smells that were wafting from each
    café door,
Were a promise that wonderful meals were in
    store.
And the growl in his stomach became a loud
    roar!
So he opened a door and went in.

It wasn't the place for a cat like himself
He thought, as he flew out the door.
For the waiter who'd stepped on his serpentine
    tail
Had dropped all the food, as he let out a wail,
And the diners who sat there were looking
    quite pale.
Not to mention the dreadful décor!

Undeterred by his first relocation attempt,
Bosley's nose told him where next to look.
This time as he stopped by a Sea Food Café
He knew that he'd found where he wanted to
    stay.
So he opened the door without further delay
And presented himself to the cook.

Now the cook was a man with a very soft
    heart
And he couldn't turn Bosley away.
So he gave him a meal on his very own dish
Full of oysters and prawns and the best kind
    of fish.
A feast that a gourmet like Bosley would wish.
With the promise of more the next day.

But back at his home things were really quite
    grim
For his owners were missing their pet.
And they'd printed up posters to put round
    the street
With a picture of Bosley, angelic and sweet.
And a promise to serve him the very best
    meat
If he'd only forgive and forget.

So Bosley the cat now has visiting rights
At the Sea Food Café up the way.
'Though he spends winter nights on a rug by
    the fire
And his owners give in to his every desire,
He can often be seen strolling up to inquire
What the café is serving today.

MINI TEST 28

For questions **1–6**, choose the option (**A**, **B**, **C** or **D**) which you think best answers the question.

1 Bosley left home because he
  A knew he would get a fish meal at the Sea Food Café.
  B was dismayed at being presented with tinned fish at home.
  C could smell good food wafting through a café door.
  D had his tail stepped on by a waiter.

2 Bosley is said to have 'followed his nose'. What does this phrase mean?
  A doing what you think is right
  B going forward purposely
  C being guided by pleasant smells
  D holding your head high

3 What happened to Bosley at the first restaurant he entered?
  A He was fed fish from a tin.
  B The growl in his stomach became a roar.
  C A waiter stood on his tail.
  D His picture went up on a poster.

4 Bosley's owners' attitude towards Bosley changed from
  A thoughtless to over-indulgent.
  B callous to indifferent.
  C apathetic to demanding.
  D responsible to suspicious.

5 What is the order of events for Bosley in the poem?
  1 Bosley is ejected from a fine café.
  2 Bosley snubs his nose at tinned fish.
  3 Bosley is a regular visitor at the Sea Food Café.
  4 Bosley's owners make Wanted posters.

  A 3, 4, 2, 1
  B 2, 1, 3, 4
  C 2, 1, 4, 3
  D 3, 4, 1, 2

6 Smells that are 'wafting' are smells that
  A get stronger and stronger.
  B cause the eyes to water.
  C are hard to distinguish.
  D pass gently through the air.

Read the extract from the poem below by Roald Dahl then answer the questions.

Television

The most important thing we've learned,
So far as children are concerned,
Is never, NEVER, NEVER let
Them near your television set—
Or better still, just don't install
The idiotic thing at all.
In almost every house we've been,
We've watched them gaping at the screen.

They loll and slop and lounge about,
And stare until their eyes pop out.
(Last week in someone's place we saw
A dozen eyeballs on the floor.)
They sit and stare and stare and sit
Until they're hypnotised by it,
Until they're absolutely drunk
With all that shocking ghastly junk.

Oh yes, we know it keeps them still,
They don't climb out the window-sill,
They never fight or kick or punch,
They leave you free to cook the lunch
And wash the dishes in the sink—
But did you ever stop to think,
To wonder just exactly what
This does to your beloved tot?

IT ROTS THE SENSE IN THE HEAD!
IT KILLS IMAGINATION DEAD!
IT CLOGS AND CLUTTERS UP THE MIND!
IT MAKES A CHILD SO DULL AND BLIND
HE CAN NO LONGER UNDERSTAND
A FANTASY, A FAIRYLAND!
HIS BRAIN BECOMES AS SOFT AS
     CHEESE!
HIS POWERS OF THINKING RUST AND
     FREEZE!
HE CANNOT THINK—HE ONLY SEES!

Source: https://allpoetry.com/poem/8503169-Television-by-Roald-Dahl

■ For questions **1–6**, choose the option (**A**, **B**, **C** or **D**) which you think best answers the question.

1 The poem is most likely intended to
   A amuse with outlandish observations.
   B reflect on the downfall of society.
   C act as a warning for parents.
   D provide beneficial advice for children.

2 How does the poet feel about children's obsession with watching television?
   A affronted   **B** bewildered
   C mortified   **D** indifferent

3 Hyperbole is a term used to describe exaggeration in literature.
   Which of these lines from the poem is an example of hyperbole?
   A They don't climb out the window-sill,
   B We've watched them gaping at the screen.
   C They leave you free to cook the lunch
   D A dozen eyeballs on the floor.)

4 What is indicated by the words 'NEVER, NEVER' in uppercase letters?
   A It increases the rhythm in that line of the poem.
   B It creates an ease of comprehension.
   C It indicates a strong emotional reaction.
   D It assists readers in their appreciation of the poem.

5 Which of these lines from the poem is an example of a simile?
   A Until they're hypnotised by it,
   B HIS BRAIN BECOMES AS SOFT AS CHEESE!
   C They loll and slop and lounge about,
   D With all that shocking ghastly junk.

6 The poet believes the children of today will
   A become extremely well informed and articulate.
   B lose their senses of sight and hearing.
   C acquire the skills to be future leaders.
   D be unable to function in a learning environment.

15 MIN

Read the poem below by Henry Lawson then answer the questions.

The Blue Mountains

Above the ashes* straight and tall,
Through ferns with moisture dripping,
I climb beneath the sandstone wall,
My feet on mosses slipping.

Like ramparts round the valley's edge
The tinted cliffs are standing,
With many a broken wall and ledge,
And many a rocky landing.

And round about their rugged feet
Deep ferny dells are hidden
In shadowed depths, whence dust and heat
Are banished and forbidden.

The stream that, crooning to itself,
Comes down a tireless rover,
Flows calmly to the rocky shelf,
And there leaps bravely over.

Now pouring down, now lost in spray
When mountain breezes sally,
The water strikes the rock midway,
And leaps into the valley.

Now in the west the colours change,
The blue with crimson blending;
Behind the far Dividing Range,
The sun is fast descending.

And mellowed day comes o'er the place,
And softens ragged edges;
The rising moon's great placid face
Looks gravely o'er the ledges.

*Type of forest tree

For questions **1–6**, choose the option (**A**, **B**, **C** or **D**) which you think best answers the question.

1 Which two words best relate to the place the poet is describing?
A slippery and dangerous
B rocky and noisy
C dusty and hot
D moist and dim

2 What is the poet referring when he writes of 'the sandstone wall'?
A a dam wall on a river
B a natural cliff face
C the ramparts of a castle
D the banks of a stream

3 In the last stanzas the poet is describing
A the coming of twilight.
B the colours of the tinted cliffs.
C the changing colour of the mountains.
D the complexion of the sandstone rock.

4 Which line from the poem is an example of personification?
A Now in the west the colours change,
B My feet on mosses slipping.
C The rising moon's great placid face
D The water strikes the rock midway,

5 The term 'leaps into the valley' is referring to
A a tireless rover.
B the deepening shadows of sunset.
C a view behind the Dividing Range.
D the waterfall.

6 What is hidden at the base of the cliff?
A ferns
B rocks
C a stream
D mosses

Read the text below then answer the questions.

Six sentences have been removed from the text. Choose from the sentences (**A–G**) the one which fits each gap (**1–6**). There is one extra sentence which you do not need to use.

Mountains

Mountains are elevated portions of the Earth's crust, generally with steep sides. People often visit them for enjoyment but mountains are also complex ecosystems. They provide diverse resources, such as food, water, and energy, for over half the population worldwide! **1** _____
Unfortunately, there are many threats to mountain habitats. It is crucial to identify the threats and to find solutions to them.

It was found that 'outsiders' pose the greatest threat to mountain ecosystems. These ecosystems are best managed by local communities based on their own community needs.

Data was collected on the environments of over fifty different mountains. **2** _____

1 mountains where the local population managed the resources according to their own needs

2 mountains where most resources were managed according to people living far from the mountains.

Mountains are ecosystems made up of different plants, animals and human populations. Depending on how a mountain is formed, it is used in different ways by the people living there. Some mountain areas are used for growing crops, while others are better for raising livestock. Some are used for extracting natural resources like water, wood and minerals. **3** _____
They enjoy activities such as hiking, biking and camping.

Because of their height and topography, mountains are often hard to get to, which can create challenges for the local populations. The local residents are usually the ones who extract and manage the rich mountain resources. However, many of the resources found in mountains are transported to other places rather than being used locally. For example, trees might be used to make houses in big cities far from the mountains.

Mountains are not only rich in resources for human use but are also very valuable for nature itself. Many different plants and animals live in mountain areas and nowhere else, such as mountain goats. **4** _____. Human populations living in the mountains help preserve these unique places and have become a valuable part of the mountain ecosystems.

Unfortunately there are hazards. **5** _____ Climate change, which creates weather extremes, often leads to damaging events. Mountains are also vulnerable to changes in policy decisions outside of the mountain regions, which can have a direct influence on the local environment and mountain communities. To sustain mountains, along with their plants, animals and resources, it is important to identify the most critical threats to our mountains and find solutions to reduce them.

Mountains are also complex ecosystems. These ecosystems are best managed by local communities based on their local needs. **6** _____

Adapted from Screen et al, 2021, How can we keep our mountains healthy?, *Science journal for kids:* https://sciencejournalforkids.org/wp-content/uploads/2021/03/Sustainable_mountains_article.pdf

---

A Snow can often cover the peaks of mountains.

B It separated them into two groups.

C Tourists also like to visit mountains.

D Without mountains, everyday life would not be sustainable for long.

E These people know their mountains.

F This makes mountain systems exceptionally beautiful habitats.

G Wildfires, landslides, avalanches and floods can affect mountain landscapes.

Read the text below then answer the questions.

Six sentences have been removed from the text. Choose from the sentences (**A–G**) the one which fits each gap (**1–6**). There is one extra sentence which you do not need to use.

Muttaburrasaurus

Muttaburrasaurus langdoni roamed the Australian landscape about 100 million years ago. The dinosaur is known from three specimens from central Queensland. **1** _____

Bones from *Muttaburrasaurus* were first discovered in 1963 by a grazier. The discovery site was on flood plains about 5 km south-east of the town of Muttaburra.

2 _____This was transported to Brisbane. It took years of painstaking work to piece the bones together and study of the animal is still incomplete.

From the reconstruction it was deduced that *Muttaburrasaurus* was about 7 m long from snout to tail. It could walk on its hind legs but spent most of its time browsing on all fours.

Muttaburrasaurus belonged to the ornithopod group of dinosaurs. **3** _____ They were plant-eating dinosaurs that walked on their hind legs. Ornithopods were known as beaked dinosaurs because they had horny beaks instead of teeth.

Muttaburrasaurus had a 15-cm-long spiked thumb on each hand used as a defensive weapon.

A distinctive feature of *Muttaburrasaurus* was an inflated, hollow, bony chamber in the animal's snout. The bones in this area were much thinner than the rest of the skull and there were at least two internal partitions, one on each side of the head. Scientists do not know why the chamber existed. **4** _____

MINI TEST 32

- the chamber may have enhanced the animal's sense of smell
- it may have been a resonating chamber, enabling the animal to make a lot of noise.

Scientists have no real idea of the environment in which *Muttaburrasaurus* lived because all three specimens from Queensland have been found in an area that was once covered by a vast inland sea.

One feature that sets *Muttaburrasaurus* apart from other ornithopods was its distinctive teeth. In other dinosaurs, and many reptiles such as crocodiles today, the teeth are replaced one by one so that the bite line is uneven on either jaw. **5** _____ When the animal's mouth was closed, the teeth came together in such a way that they acted like a pair of shears.

The back of the skull was also significantly larger than other related dinosaurs. This increased area would have been covered with a larger amount of muscle tissue, which gave *Muttaburrasaurus* a stronger bite.

The increased muscle power, together with the shearing action of the teeth, suggests *Muttaburrasaurus* fed on tougher plants than other herbivorous dinosaurs. **6** _____

Adapted from *Muttaburrasaurus by* Ralph Molnar, Queensland Museum Learning, 2011

A   There are several possibilities:

B   Perhaps it ate the spiky fonds of cycads.

C   A museum team collected five tonnes of rock material from the site.

D   No bones of meat-eating dinosaurs have, as yet, been discovered.

E   Ornithopods have been found worldwide and lived from over 65 million years ago.

F   It is believed to have been common during the early Cretaceous Period.

G   In *Muttaburrasaurus* the teeth were all replaced at the same time, so the upper and lower jaws fitted together evenly.

Read the text below then answer the questions.

Six sentences have been removed from the text. Choose from the sentences (**A–G**) the one which fits each gap (**1–6**). There is one extra sentence which you do not need to use.

The Era of the Mutants

He was a man but looked more like some Neanderthal than a Homo sapiens of the 21st century. It was hard to distinguish just what was hair and what was rudimentary clotheskins as he ducked around the giant concrete pillars that had once supported a railway and an expressway. The structure was still in place but now both road and track were silent. **1** _____

The hunched being slunk furtively out from the early morning shadows and made his way towards the crumbling concrete wall that edged the harbour. He stepped warily down over the large broken blocks. **2** _____ Pieces of rusted reinforcing steel rods pointed in an array of directions like the spikes of some immobile sea mine. As he reached the water's edge he looked over his shoulder towards the deserted and ransacked buildings under the ancient expressway. Nothing moved.

He quickly found his line, weathered electrical cable, that was secured to a steel beam. He pulled slowly. A small, crude fish trap broke the surface of the green water. He had long forgotten the skill of fishing with a line that the elders had taught him.

He let out a soft grunt of pleasure as he examined the catch and jabbered excitedly. It was not unlike the English of the decaying signs that had once adorned Circular Quay.

The mutant-fish were small and bloated. Their heads were misshapen and their eyes were covered with a light film. Pinkish, soft tumours hung to the underbelly. **3** _____

A gurgling gasp came from the largest fish. The being was suddenly wary, thoughtful. Was it a bad sign, an ill omen? But the fish was also food.

The being deftly tied his catch to twine around his waist, threw his trap back into the harbour and retreated up the concrete blocks. He quickly surveyed the expressway shadows between the two tunnels. **4** _____ No packs lurking by deserted buildings. And there were the deformed loners hidden in overgrown parks. All were predators coveting any scraps he might have collected.

Then there were the hordes of hungry, vicious, outsized mutant cats.

The man was also vaguely preoccupied with the meeting the tribe was to have shortly. **5** _____

He coughed and braced himself against stabs of pain in his chest.

As he looked across the water he could see a half-submerged Shark Cat ferry. The sun was rising above the horizon. **6** _____

A   Nothing moved but he was still cautious.

B   Recent meetings had ended more in division than unity.

C   Grotesque creatures roamed the derelict streets after dark.

D   The first insipid rays struck the top floors of the grimy skyscrapers.

E   They were slippery with a thin coating of noisome slime.

F   The fins were uneven and broken.

G   Dead arteries of a once-throbbing metropolitan transport system.

MINI TEST 34: Narrative

20 MIN

Read the text below then answer the questions.

Six sentences have been removed from the text. Choose from the sentences (**A–G**) the one which fits each gap (**1–6**). There is one extra sentence which you do not need to use.

The Martians Arrive

The huge metallic saucer lay half-buried in its crash crater.

The top of a cylinder was being screwed out of the top from within. Nearly a metre of shining screw projected. I blinked, and as I did, the screw made its last rotation. **1** _____ I kept my eyes on the saucer. For a moment that circular cavity seemed perfectly black. I had the sunset in my eyes.

Everyone expected to see a man emerge—possibly something not unlike us but essentially human. I did. Watching, I saw something stirring within the shadows: greyish billowy movements and then two luminous disks like eyes. Then something resembling a little grey snake, as thick as a walking stick, coiled up out of the writhing middle and wriggled in the air towards me—and then another.

A sudden chill came over me. **2** _____ I half turned, keeping my eyes on the saucer as more tentacles emerged. I edged back from the crater. I saw astonishment giving way to horror on the faces of the people nearby. I heard gasps on all sides. There was a general movement backwards. **3** _____ I looked again at the saucer and, gripped with terror, I stood gaping.

A big greyish rounded bulk, the size of a bear, was rising slowly and painfully out of the saucer. **4** _____

Two large dark-coloured eyes regarded me steadfastly. The mass that framed them, the head of the thing, was rounded and had, one might say, a face. There was a mouth under the eyes, the lipless brim of which quivered and dropped saliva. The whole creature heaved and pulsated convulsively.

5 _____ The peculiar V-shaped mouth with its pointed upper lip, the absence of brow ridges, the absence of a chin beneath the wedgelike lower lip, the incessant quivering of this mouth, the tumultuous breathing of the lungs in a strange atmosphere, the evident heaviness and painfulness of movement due to Earth's greater gravity—above all, the intensity of the immense eyes—were at once vital, intense, inhuman, crippled and monstrous. There was something fungoid in the oily brown skin, something in the clumsy deliberation of the tedious movements unspeakably nasty. Even with this first glimpse, I was overcome with disgust and dread.

6 _____ It had toppled over the saucer's brim and fallen into the crater as another creature appeared in the gloom of the aperture.

Adapted from *War of the Worlds* by HG Wells

A There was a loud shriek from a woman behind me.

B The lid of the cylinder fell onto the gravel with a ringing concussion.

C I found myself alone and saw people on the other side of the crater running off.

D Suddenly the monster vanished.

E As it bulged up and caught the light, it glistened like wet leather.

F Those who have never seen a living Martian can scarcely imagine the strange horror of its appearance.

G How they reached this part of England we will never know.

Read the text below then answer the questions.

Six sentences have been removed from the text. Choose from the sentences (**A–G**) the one which fits each gap (**1–6**). There is one extra sentence which you do not need to use.

Aerial Encounter

Two shadows winged across the desert landscape as the sun began its burning afternoon descent. **1** _____ It was more a meandering in wide, lazy curves towards the perimeter security fence.

Occasionally a startled kangaroo would hop from its meagre shade then look towards the bleached sky.

One shadow led the way while the second was in a persistent game of catch-up.

2 _____ Its glossy black surface caught the light as it weaved its way on a course directed from relay stations set strategically along the formidable outer fence.

Its four whirring rotors were powered by powerful batteries and housed beneath was an atomic solar charger. The drone could cruise constantly while the sun shone and had enough battery reserve for another three hours after sunset—enough for its return to base.

The Quadrone flew no higher than eight metres. The height of the perimeter fence was five metres, including the top collar of electrified razor wire. **3** _____

The drone slipped across the landscape, rising and falling with every change in the terrain with its blue-grey saltbush and dry, bristly spinifex cushions which dotted the landscape of sand or gibbers with soft yellow-grey clumps. All the time it cruised under possible radar detection but it created alarm in the small animals that were venturing out from holes or hummocks of dry desert grasses to feed.

MINI TEST 35

Back at base a young engineer watched on monitors as the landscape slipped by. **4** _____ The drone adjusted its flight path.

The second shadow was that of a predator cruising thirty metres above its quarry.

It was an agitated wedge-tailed eagle that had been disturbed from its perch on a leafless tree struggling among a scattering of boulders, like headstones in a vandalised graveyard.

The wedge-tail had a distinctive tail, like the shape of a US Raptor—a lethal fighter jet. Its legs were feathered, down to the razor-sharp talons that could pierce the hide of any desert mammal. The talons were a deadly complement to its powerful hooked beak that could rip through flesh. **5** _____

The whirr of the passing of the drone was an omen. The eagle's territory had an unexpected intruder.

The wedge-tail dropped from its eerie before finding thermals above the hot plain and rising high above the shimmering sand and rock. With its keen eyesight it could position itself to dive on the intruder at breakneck speed.

6 _____ As the drone approached the perimeter fence it turned towards the sinking sun.

A   The eagle stalked the drone.

B   An ALL CLEAR signal beeped.

C   This four-kilogram adult male was a formidable attacking machine.

D   Quadrones were a common sight above this remote desert landscape.

E   The route from a distant rocky hillock was not a straight line.

F   A safety margin of just a few metres.

G   The first shadow was created by a Quadrone on a routine surveillance mission.

Read the text below then answer the questions.

Six sentences have been removed from the text. Choose from the sentences (**A–G**) the one which fits each gap (**1–6**). There is one extra sentence which you do not need to use.

Rock climbing

Are you afraid of heights? Rock climbing is a recreational activity in which athletes climb up, down and across natural rock formations. Hiking and camping are great ways to connect with nature. **1** _____ Despite the heights, climbers enjoy this peaceful environment. As a result, the number of people using cliffs has increased rapidly.

Cliff ecosystems are the homes of many living things, especially birds. Since climbing is a fairly new activity we don't know its impact on cliff ecosystems.

2 _____ An obvious reaction is: it doesn't. Rocks are not living. However, cliffs provide habitats and protection for lots of creatures. Some living things found in cliff habitats are special. They have features that help them survive there which are not found anywhere else. Certain birds are special in this way. They make their nests and only forage from cliffs.

3 _____ However, it is not known how climbing impacts on different birds living together on a cliff because climbing is a newly popular activity and cliff environments are difficult for researchers to reach. They wanted to know how climbing affects whole bird communities, not just raptor species. The raptor group (birds of prey) includes eagles, falcons, owls and hawks.

Selected cliff faces were watched and records were taken by the scientist and researchers as to how many birds were observed and what the species were. Records of climbers that were in the cliffs were also kept. Hour-long observations were conducted several times a day over many days. This was tedious work. It required patience.

The results were informative. The diversity of birds was highest on east-facing cliffs and the lowest on west-facing cliffs. The abundance of birds was also highest on the east-facing cliffs. **4** _____ The diversity of bird types was higher where there were no climbers. That meant that climbers scare away some species of birds.

Overall, the research concluded that rock climbing doesn't impact so much on bird numbers but on the diversity of birds using the cliff. However, the way the cliff faces also has a major influence on both diversity and how many birds use the cliff. **5** _____ On some cliffs that were used a lot for climbing, bird abundance was very high. This suggests that some species put up with human intrusion quite well. South-facing cliffs have fewer species. **6** _____

Adapted from *How does rock climbing impact birds?*:
https://sciencejournalforkids.org/wp-content/uploads/2021/03/Sustainable_mountains_article.pdf

A   Not only were there more birds on these cliffs but more birds of each type.

B   Another outdoor activity, rock climbing, has become very popular.

C   Many birds nest in inaccessible places.

D   Early studies have shown how climbers disturb nesting birds such as raptors.

E   East-facing cliffs have the highest while west-facing cliffs have the lowest.

F   How does climbing impact the cliff environment?

G   Enjoy the cliffs but respect the wildlife.

Read the text below then answer the questions.

Six sentences have been removed from the text. Choose from the sentences (**A–G**) the one which fits each gap (**1–6**). There is one extra sentence which you do not need to use.

Lost

An insipid moon ventured from behind heavy clouds, casting eerie shadows through the seemingly impenetrable scrub.

A dog barked in the distance. Then another. **1** _____ Can't be for protection.

Then gun shots. Not target practice! He didn't want to be mistaken for a feral pig scrambling through the scrub.

Yuri desperately pushed his way through the darkening undergrowth. He was going downhill, towards the river—too quickly. Blackthorns scratched his face and lashed his arms but he pushed on, ignoring the pain.

A tangle of unseen thorny vines ripped viciously at his ankles. Suddenly he stumbled and crashed against a small sapling. **2** _____ He worried about the dogs. He listened. There seemed to be dogs barking all across the valley. It only took one old hound to slip its leash to find his trail.

Fear became real, fluid. He was in a black ocean of fear. Shadowy tree branches loomed over his shaking body like grasping arms.

More gun shots and excited barking from along the riverbed. **3** _____ A cold shiver ran down his spine. He pressed on. The ground became steeper. The soil underfoot was no longer hard but soft, giving. It was sandy!

Yuri suddenly realised he was heading down the riverbank. Any moment now he could be sliding into the water or tumbling onto jumbled rocks. He backtracked cautiously. **4** _____ He knew then that he had missed the clearing. He had no idea of which way to turn. He was reluctant to retrace his steps back up the slope. Farm dogs were still barking across the otherwise silent valley. He could see no farmhouse lights.

Yuri swallowed hard and turned. He knew in his panic he must have crossed the narrow walking track to the camp site. If he could find it, he'd have a reference point.

He forged on, blocking out fears that he was totally lost.

Suddenly there was another burst of barking. **5** _____ Too close!

He knew now. If he went further downstream he could stumble off a cliff into the black evening waters of Devil's Hell Hole to be ensnared in a tangle of submerged uprooted trees. He shuddered at the thought.

Then Yuri stood stock still, his ears straining. He didn't know how long he had been on the run. **6** _____

Adapted from *The Mind of Yuri Kirakov* by Alan Horsfield (unpublished)

A Dead trees silhouetted against the sky seemed to reach out for Yuri.

B He could just make out the tops of tall riverbank casuarinas against a velvet sky studded with stars.

C It came from somewhere along the shadowy, sandy riverbed.

D He picked himself up and waited to catch his breath.

E Then Yuri remembered how well dogs could ruthlessly follow scent trails.

F It seemed ages.

G Why do people in the country have so many dogs?

Read the text below then answer the questions.

Six sentences have been removed from the text. Choose from the sentences (**A–G**) the one which fits each gap (**1–6**). There is one extra sentence which you do not need to use.

Oranges!

Oranges are a round, segmented citrus fruit with a pitted peel. The taste can vary from juicy and sweet to bitter, depending on the variety. Most oranges are available year-round, except for varieties such as blood oranges. **1** _____

Oranges are known for Vitamin C and health-promoting compounds. Orange peel actually contains more nutrients than the flesh! Oranges are a great fruit.

However, in Spain ...

There are over 48 000 orange trees that spread through all corners of Seville, Spain. They not only fill the city's air with the pleasant smell of Azhar perfume, or orange blossom, in spring, they also yield over 16 000 tonnes of fruit every winter. That gives the Seville region the right to claim it is Europe's top orange-producing region. **2** _____ While some of the produce is used to make marmalade and orange liqueur, most of it ends up in Seville's landfills. That may change soon thanks to an ingenious idea to use the oranges to produce clean energy.

The pilot program is being launched by the city's Council and Parks Department in collaboration with Seville's water supply and sanitation division (Emasesa). **3** _____ The methane gas released from the fermented liquid will be captured and used to drive a generator to produce clean

power. The officials estimate the test run will generate enough energy to run one of Emasesa's water purification plants. **4** _____

Benigno López, the head of Emasesa's environmental department, said, 'It's not just about saving money. **5** _____ We're producing benefits from waste'.

If successful, the city hopes to recycle all the oranges and add the electricity generated back to its grid. In trial runs, 1000 kilos of oranges produced 50 kWh of clean energy. **6** _____ The project team estimates that if all the fruit is recycled, it will produce enough energy to power as many as 73 000 homes.

Emasesa is now a role model in Spain for sustainability and the fight against climate change. This project will help Spain to reach its targets for reducing harmful emissions and energy self-sufficiency. The latest endeavour is among the many steps being taken across Spain to achieve the country's goal of switching its electricity system from fossil fuels to renewable sources by 2050.

Still, it's a good idea to keep a bowl on the counter stocked with fresh oranges.

Adapted from https://www.dogonews.com

A   The oranges are a big problem for the city.

B   Juice extracted from 38.6 tonnes of oranges will be left to ferment in an existing biogas facility.

C   To ensure there is no waste the orange skins, peels and pulp will be used as fertiliser.

D   That's enough to fulfil the daily electricity needs of five homes.

E   Officials hope the scheme is successful.

F   They have a shorter season.

G   However, the fruit is much too tart to be consumed fresh!

Read the text below then answer the questions.

Six sentences have been removed from the text. Choose from the sentences (**A–G**) the one which fits each gap (**1–6**). There is one extra sentence which you do not need to use.

Penguins

As we drew near to the island we were amused by the manoeuvres and appearance of many strange birds. They seemed to be different species. Some had crests on their heads while others had none. Some were about the size of a goose; others as large as a swan. We also saw a huge albatross soaring above the heads of the penguins. We approached within a few yards of the island, which was a low rock with a few bushes, and watched the birds with pleasure. **1** _____

We now saw that the penguins' soldier-like appearance was owing to the stiff, erect manner in which they sat on their short legs. They had black heads, long sharp beaks, white breasts and bluish backs. **2** _____ We soon saw that they used them to swim under water.

There were no quills on these wings but a sort of scaly feathers, which also covered their bodies. Their legs were short and placed so far back that the birds, while on land, had to stand upright to keep their balance. In the water they floated like other water birds.

3 _____ They covered the rocks in thousands. As we watched, we observed several quadrupeds (as we thought) walking among the penguins.

'Pull in a bit,' cried Peterkin, 'and let's see what these are. They must enjoy noisy company.'

To our surprise we found these were penguins which had gone down on all fours. **4** _____

Suddenly one big old bird that had been sitting on a point near to us became alarmed, scuttled down the rocks, then plumped rather than ran into the sea. **5** _____ Immediately it plunged back into the sea. We could scarcely believe it was not a fish that had made the leap.

'That beats everything,' said Peterkin, screwing up his face with an expression of amazement. 'I've heard of a thing being neither fish, flesh, nor fowl but I never did expect to live to see all in one! But look there!' he continued, pointing to the shore. 'There's no end to it. What has that one got under its tail?'

We looked in the direction he pointed. **6** _____ We found later that this species of penguins always carried their eggs that way.

Adapted from *The Coral Island* by RM Ballantyne

A	There we saw a penguin walking slowly and very sedately along the shore with an egg under its tail.
B	The rock was covered in discarded feathers.
C	Their wings were so short that they looked more like the fins of a fish.
D	They were crawling among the rocks on their feet and wings, just like sea mammals.
E	We were stunned by the incessant noise from the birds.
F	They returned our gaze with curiosity.
G	It dived under the surface and many long seconds later shot out of the water someway off.

Read the four texts below on the theme of Australian towns.

For questions **1–10**, choose the option (**A**, **B**, **C** or **D**) which you think best answers the question.

Which text ...

describes a town that produces a variety of food products?	**1**	_____
refers to a town that was purpose built?	**2**	_____
mentions being able to see preserved relics of equipment that were in use in the 1880s?	**3**	_____
compares visitors' impressions of the town to what locals see as mundane?	**4**	_____
names a town that is a great distance from the next town west?	**5**	_____
states that a reason for visiting the town is its connection with military history?	**6**	_____
mentions a place whose name does **not** have a First Nations Australian connection?	**7**	_____
describes a town that no longer functions as a population centre?	**8**	_____
explains why a town had a subtle name change?	**9**	_____
discusses some harsh conditions that visitors will encounter?	**10**	_____

TEXT A

Ceduna is the one major township on the eastern side of the Great Australian Bight. It is located 776 km north-west of Adelaide via Port Augusta and 1200 km to the east of Norseman in Western Australia. Population 2100.

Other than the WA border 480 km away, all that lies between the two towns (Norseman and Ceduna) are roadhouses which provide food, accommodation and fuel for those crossing the Nullarbor Plain. Ceduna is really the last easterly stop before entering the arid Nullarbor Plain and the vast flatlands north of the Great Australian Bight.

It is an attractive town which, with the nearby port of Thevenard, is located on Murat Bay which in turn is part of the larger Denial Bay. It is a vibrant multicultural community with a significant First Nations Australian population.

The service centre for a rural area known for its agriculture (predominantly grain and sheep), salt and gypsum mining, and seafood—particularly oysters—Ceduna is set amidst a patchwork of grain farms, natural bush and rugged rocky bays, secluded white sandy beaches and wilderness.

The name Ceduna is probably a corruption of the local Wirangu word chedoona which possibly means 'a place to sit down and rest'.

Adapted from https://www.aussietowns.com.au/town/ceduna-sa

TEXT B

Woomera is an artificial town specifically designed by the Long-Range Weapons Board of Administration to provide accommodation and facilities for personnel—scientists, technicians and ancillary staff—who came to work at an isolated experimental station which was used to test rockets, weapons and missiles. It is located in the South Australian desert 500 km north of Adelaide and 165 m above sea level.

During the 1960s Woomera had a population of over 5000. Today the population is around 120. Over the years it has changed from being an important location for experimenting with rockets— which, at various times, has been used by NASA and the armed forces of Australia, Great Britain, the US and West Germany—to being a curiosity.

Between 1999 and 2003 it was used by the Australian Government as an Immigration Detention Centre. It housed asylum seekers who had arrived in Australia by sea.

Today Woomera township is open to the public. Its main appeal is the Woomera Heritage Centre and the Missile Park.

Woomera is a Dharug word for a type of throwing stick with a notch at one end for holding a dart or spear, thus giving increased leverage in throwing.

Adapted from https://www.aussietowns.com.au/town/woomera-sa

TEXT C

Prior to the arrival of Europeans, the area around Mossman was home to the Kuku Yalanji people.

Mossman is located 1760 km north of Brisbane on the Bruce Highway. It is 21 km north-west of Port Douglas and has a population of 1900.

Like many hinterland towns in Far North Queensland, Mossman leads a Cinderella-like existence. It has two significant attractions: in the sugar-cane harvesting season the trains bringing sugar cane to the mill actually travel down the main street (an unforgettable sight for visitors—very 'unspecial' for locals) and the Mossman Gorge, a genuinely beautiful stretch of tropical rainforest where local First Nations Australians can introduce visitors to traditional culture and which is the gateway to the world's oldest rainforest, the Daintree Rainforest. The town has some interesting historic buildings but basically it's a town in the shadow of the attractive coastal beaches and the tourist charm of Port Douglas.

Mossman was named by the explorer George Dalrymple in 1873 after Hugh Mosman who found gold at Charters Towers in 1872! It is amusing that Mossman changed its spelling because of confusion with the suburb Mosman in Sydney.

Adapted from https://www.aussietowns.com.au/town/mossman-qld

TEXT D

Arltunga is a fascinating rarity: a gold-rush ghost town in the middle of some of the harshest Australian desert. It is worth visiting because the climate has held much of the old town intact. The visitor can easily imagine life during the first gold rush and the subsequent period when government works were operating. Curious visitors can see pieces of meat safes, rusted wire, rusted cans and shards of broken glass littering the ground.

Arltunga lacked water, had limited supplies of basic foods, suffered extremes of temperature and the cost of living was exorbitant. Now a 120-km drive from Alice Springs, to reach Arltunga in the 1880s prospectors had to walk or ride alongside the Overland Telegraph Line from Oodnadatta to Alice Springs, then follow the MacDonnell Ranges east for around 120 km. This would take at least a week, longer in 40 °C temperatures.

Fresh vegetables could not be grown. Limited water supplies were drawn from wells and water soaks in creeks. High food costs were passed onto the Arltunga residents, including First Nations Australians, miners, publicans, stockmen and pastoralists.

The town was named after the Arrernte people who had lived in the desert area for tens of thousands of years before the brief mining boom that established the town.

Adapted from:
https://www.thrillist.com.au/travel/best-abandoned-towns-australia
https://www.aussietowns.com.au/town/arltunga

Read the four texts below on the theme of orchards.

For questions **1–10**, choose the option (**A**, **B**, **C** or **D**) which you think best answers the question.

Which text ...

refers to the planting of fruit trees as an investment in the future?	**1**	_____
describes a feeling of having chanced onto something important?	**2**	_____
mentions that some children's books left out some facts to be more acceptable?	**3**	_____
argues the reasons for having orchards?	**4**	_____
has a positive expectation about fruit varieties?	**5**	_____
states that orchards can have detrimental effects on the environment?	**6**	_____
discusses the attributes of a particular variety of fruit?	**7**	_____
describes why authorities take an interest in orchards?	**8**	_____
explains that the planting of apple trees may have been done with ulterior motives?	**9**	_____
discusses some of the practicalities of farming in the late 1800s?	**10**	_____

TEXT A

If you love orchards and the delicious fruit within them as much as we do, you may have never seriously asked yourself why we should plant and nurture orchards. It turns out there are lots of great reasons justifying orchards should you ever encounter an unbeliever.

Orchards have played an important role in small communities for many centuries, providing a focal point, a gathering space and a place where people and the rest of nature successfully work together to create abundant harvests, providing fresh fruit long before the time of global freight.

Along the way many customs and traditions have developed, as have thousands of different variaties of fruit. As with the well-known apple, each cultivar with its unique flavour, texture, use and story, links people to place and heritage.

As small orchards gave way to extensive farms, unique varieties along with the skills used to produce them were lost. Now most of the world's commercially grown fruits all come from a limited number of parent varieties. Luckily though, in recent years, community orchards have had a renaissance as people rediscover the benefits and pleasures of growing fresh fruit from trees.

Adapted from theorchardproject.org.uk

TEXT B

An orchard is defined as land consisting of a small, cultivated wood without undergrowth and typically incorporates fruit or nuts. These are diverse and include cool climate varieties, Mediterranean climate species and tropical species.

Orchards are a long-standing and valued contributor to the wellbeing of the community and State economy. Like other industries, they need to operate in harmony with the environment to ensure their sustainability and community support. Orchards conducted intensively without barriers to prevent chemical leaching into the environment can pose a threat to the quality of water resources. Threats may arise from chemical leaching driven by over-watering, excessive or poorly timed use of fertilisers or pesticides, soil erosion, inappropriate storage of chemicals and disposal of wastes that can leach contaminants. Pollutants can move into surface water catchments as suspended solids, bound to other sediments, or into groundwater by dissolving in water.

There are official and commercial publications that offer guidance on establishing and operating orchards within the vicinity of sensitive water resources that aim to minimise any risk of water contamination. Each species requires different conditions, inputs and management techniques to optimise crop yield while avoiding nuisance to neighbours or harm to the environment.

Adapted from https://www.water.wa.gov.au

TEXT C

Surprisingly, one of the most notable businessmen of the American frontier didn't wear traditional clothes but rather dressed in a coffee sack, donned a tin hat and travelled barefoot. John Chapman, better known as Johnny Appleseed, was a 19th-century horticulturist who made great contributions to the westward expansion of the United States. Chapman paved the way for countless new settlements around his orchards.

Chapman, the son of a farmer, was born in 1774 in Massachusetts. He moved to Ohio, bringing seeds from Pennsylvania cider presses with him and planting them along the way. Though his legend may paint a picture of Johnny Appleseed planting at random and selflessly handing out seeds to needy settlers, his path followed a commonsense plan. Children's books about Appleseed have removed talk of alcohol from the story but Chapman's success was centred not around fresh apples but rather the cider they could create. Cider was a dinner-table beverage at the time, so most homes had their own small orchard. Chapman planted orchards along the pioneers' routes, staying ahead of competition since his nomadic, unmarried lifestyle allowed him to cover more ground. He then traded his seedlings with new settlers in the area so they could grow apples for cider.

Adapted from https://www.history.com/news/who-was-johnny-appleseed

TEXT D

The Granny Smith apple had its origin in an orchard near Sydney.

Maria Ann Smith arrived in Australia with husband Thomas in 1830 aged 30. She already had three children when they established their family home and orchard in Epping.

Maria was the driving force of her family and when her fruiting trees were bearing and there were sufficient vegetables and eggs she would rent a stall at the City Markets. She would often buy other fruit to take back home.

On one such occasion Maria bought a case of Tasmanian French crabapples. When the last of these had gone bad in the case, she dumped them by the water course that ran through their property. Some seeds germinated and produced fruit. Mrs Smith knew the apples were not French crabapples and were distinctively different to any other apple she had seen. She had something very special but now she required her new apple variety to be accepted.

In 1868 she called in a local orchardist and horticulturist to give his opinion of her apple. He identified it as a new variety.

Apples during this period were either categorised as being good for eating raw or best for cooking. Granny Smith's apple fulfilled both requirements!

Read the four texts below on the theme of parrots.

For questions **1–10**, choose the option (**A**, **B**, **C** or **D**) which you think best answers the question.

Which text ...

argues that breeding captive parrots may be the only way to save the species from extinction?	1	_____
reports a feeling of hope for the survival of a parrot species?	2	_____
refers to a parrot that can use a stick as a drumstick?	3	_____
describes the distinctive head features of a parrot?	4	_____
gives natural disaster as the reason for the possible extinction of this parrot species?	5	_____
states that some caged parrots are reluctant to leave the security of the cage?	6	_____
explains survival strategies of some parrot species living in harsh environments?	7	_____
describes one parrot's very distinctive call?	8	_____
explains the origin of the parrot's popular name?	9	_____
reveals the cultural significance of a parrot species?	10	_____

TEXT A

Dozens of endangered, orange-bellied parrots have been released by wildlife carers into the wild from three sites in Victoria, as part of a program to save the birds from extinction.

Several years ago there were less than 50 orange-bellied parrots, including four females, left in the wild, but a large-scale captive-breeding and release program has managed to boost numbers significantly in a few years.

The captive-bred birds took about an hour to fly from their aviaries. They did not seem to be in a hurry, stopping to eat bird food before flying away. The aviaries will be left open in case the parrots need to return for food or shelter.

It's hoped they will attract other parrots that are currently migrating to Victoria from south-west Tasmania and together the birds will establish flocks in high-quality habitats.

The parrots spend summer breeding in Tasmania, nesting in the hollows of eucalypt trees near button-grass plains. They migrate to spend winter in South Australia and Victoria, where they usually stay within 3 km of the coast.

The species has become critically endangered due to habitat loss and predation by cats and foxes. They are one of only three migratory parrot species in the world.

Adapted from https://en.wikipedia.org›wiki›Orange-bellied_parrot

---

TEXT B

The palm cockatoo, also called the goliath cockatoo, is a native to Cape York Peninsula. It has a very large black beak and prominent red cheek patches.

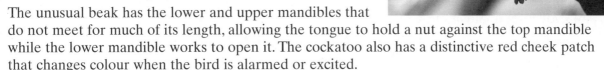

The palm cockatoo can be 60 cm in length and weigh up to 1200 g. It is a distinctive bird with a large crest and has the largest bill of any parrot. This powerful bill enables palm cockatoos not only to eat very hard nuts and seeds but also enables males to break off thick sticks from live trees to use for a drumming display.

The unusual beak has the lower and upper mandibles that do not meet for much of its length, allowing the tongue to hold a nut against the top mandible while the lower mandible works to open it. The cockatoo also has a distinctive red cheek patch that changes colour when the bird is alarmed or excited.

It has a unique territorial display where the male bird drums a large stick against a dead bough or tree, creating a noise that can be heard 100 m away. Later the male strips the stick into small pieces to line the nest.

The palm cockatoo is one of the few birds known to use tools.

Adapted from https://en.wikipedia.org/wiki/Palm_cockatoo

TEXT C

There's no question the word budgerigar (commonly abbreviated to budgie) is derived from a First Nations Australian language, albeit corrupted by clumsy colonial attempts to record it. Since the earliest inhabitants first set foot on Australian soil more than 50000 years ago, they have known the budgerigar.

As one of the creatures created by the spirits, the budgerigar ancestor also shines in the heavens of First Nations Australian astronomy and in Dreamtime storytelling.

Often seen in flocks, resembling large green tornadoes, wild budgies desperately search the vast desert landscapes of Central Australia for water during the hot, dry summer months. Research suggests they're better adapted to the harsh climate than first thought. Much like mammals, budgies can regulate the water they lose through their skin.

To witness small, seed-eating budgies in the hundreds of thousands, even millions, flashing gold and green as they twist and turn in unison to create billowing patterns in the sky, is on the must-do list of serious international birders. So enthusiastically has the budgerigar been embraced overseas as a pet and exhibition bird that many Australians may have forgotten the fact it is indeed an Australian native.

Adapted from https://www.bushheritage.org.au/species/budgerigars

TEXT D

The secretive eastern ground parrot of Australia is one of only five ground-dwelling parrots in the world, two others being its closest relatives, the western ground parrot and the extremely rare night parrot.

The ground parrot is a stunningly beautiful bird. It is a distinctive, bright grass-green, long-tailed, ground-dwelling parrot of the coastal and sub-coastal heaths, reaching 30 cm long. The green upperparts are heavily mottled with yellow and black, and the greenish-yellow underparts are barred brown. The forehead of individuals older than three or four months is orange-red. This species has a distinctive call, given at dawn and dusk, that consists of a series of piercing, resonating whistles, rising in steps, with each note flowing on almost unbroken, but abruptly higher than the preceding note. The species is rarely seen unless flushed, although birds can be seen fluttering low over heath at dusk.

Intense and extensive bushfire is a major threat to these birds; large areas of their ranges were impacted by the 2019–20 bushfires. The parrot was already an endangered species before these bushfires and so bushfire recovery is especially important. A captive-bred population may assist in recovery of the species after recent catastrophic fire events.

Adapted from https://en.wikipedia.org/wiki/Eastern_ground_parrot

Read the four texts below on the theme of rooms.

For questions **1–10**, choose the option (**A**, **B**, **C** or **D**) which you think best answers the question.

Which text ...

describes an awareness of a room left in a very orderly state?	**1**	_____
expresses the writer's disdain for the quality of the room?	**2**	_____
outlines differences in a room's function over a period of time?	**3**	_____
ponders the relative enjoyment of school activities?	**4**	_____
compares the difference between two upper-level rooms?	**5**	_____
states with certainty that a room has not been utilised recently?	**6**	_____
considers that changes in a room's function were ongoing improvements?	**7**	_____
describes a room where the peace is disturbed by a series of tapping sounds?	**8**	_____
explains the reason why a room may be uncomfortable to occupy?	**9**	_____
mentions personal belongings of a recent occupier?	**10**	_____

TEXT A

Lisa climbed the narrow stairs to the landing and dipped her head under a low beam to reach the landing. Here was a narrow passage with three doors. It was almost dark. The only light slanted up from the kitchen below.

Lisa rubbed her hands together before opening each door and checking inside. There were two small bedrooms, both with single beds, both made, and a bathroom.

She checked out the bathroom first. It was tiny with a small corner bath and a shower built over it, a basin and a lavatory. No room for a chair or a cupboard, except for a small unit fixed to the wall above the sink. Mirrored doors. Inside a wrapped bar of soap and some toothpaste. Over-the-counter medicines, remedies for colds and flu, indigestion. No sleeping tablets or headache pills. No prescription medications.

How long since the owner had showered? Lisa wondered. The bath was dry. The room seemed almost spotless. There was a faint smell of bleach and the lingering smell of some pine-scented toilet cleaner.

Adapted from *The Glass Room* by Ann Cleeves

TEXT B

Post-1960, kitchen electrical appliances and other conveniences shifted the balance of time and labour that went into feeding a family and managing a home. The freestanding wood or coal oven had finally gone! The oven's stovetop saved fuel and saved the cook from crouching.

Finally, appliances for your kitchen helped get perfect baking results every time. The kitchen clock was about to make an appearance so that cooks could—at last—time their cooking!

By the 1960s it was not just an electric fridge and gas cooker that made life easier in the kitchen. The painted or laminated surfaces and linoleum flooring made quicker work of keeping the kitchen clean—'lino' was the preferred kitchen flooring. Floor tiles were yet to come! The copper-bottom stainless-steel pans under the breakfast bar were low-maintenance. And there was a plug-in toaster and coffee percolator hidden in one of those cupboards.

Perimeter countertops freed up social space at the heart of the kitchen as food preparation became part of 'entertaining'. Designer units and utensils were all the rage. Designing, buying and using kitchenware were now expressions of consumer freedom and aspiration.

Source: https://www.nogarlicnoonions.com/500-years-of-kitchen-design-a-video-review/

TEXT C

An attic, sometimes referred to as a loft, is a space found directly below the pitched roof of a house or other building. An attic may also be called a sky parlour or a garret. Because attics fill the space between the ceiling of the top floor of a building and the slanted roof, they are known for being awkwardly shaped spaces with exposed rafters and difficult-to-reach corners.

While some attics are converted into bedrooms, home offices or attic apartments complete with windows and staircases, most remain difficult to access (and are usually entered using a loft hatch and ladder). Attics are generally used for storage, though they can also help control temperatures in a house by providing a large mass of slowly moving air. The hot air rising from the lower floors of a building is often retained in attics, further compounding their reputation as inhospitable environments.

A loft is also the uppermost space in a building but is distinguished from an attic in that an attic typically covers an entire floor of the building, while a loft covers only a few rooms, leaving one or more sides open to the lower floor.

Adapted from https://en.wikipedia.org/wiki/Attic

TEXT D

I sat in the library doing my homework. It was easier to work there than at home.

It was great in the old library, the shelves reaching up to the ceiling, big windows looking out onto the playing fields. There were window seats too and I spent many an afternoon there immersed in a pleasant fantasy horror while our first eleven lost another match to a cricket team down below.

The libraries they build now are horrible, all plastic sofas and carousels and paperbacks in protective covers. *Paperbacks!* And synthetic carpet on the floor with modernistic patterns that mean nothing.

The old libraries had history and you could feel it seeping through the walls and rising up from the floorboards, which were knotted and wide like the gangplanks of a ship.

Even the signs on the old libraries gave a reassuring familiarity to the space. QUIET PLEASE and CLOSING TIME—4:30. Now it's just the staccato tapping of keys and the electronic warning beeps of impersonal devices.

From *The Stranger Diaries* by Elly Griffiths, Hachette Australia

Read the four texts below on the theme of characters.

For questions **1–10**, choose the option (**A**, **B**, **C** or **D**) which you think best answers the question.

Which text ...

describes a feeling of disgust?	**1**	_____
refers to an incident that may have happened centuries ago?	**2**	_____
expresses the respect the writer has for the occupant of the room?	**3**	_____
indicates a person who has an appreciation for privacy in a public place?	**4**	_____
says the character involved felt a mystifying uneasiness?	**5**	_____
suggests that first impressions may have been deceiving?	**6**	_____
mentions features of a place that indicates its public purpose?	**7**	_____
describes two people totally different in appearance?	**8**	_____
alludes to a character who is somewhat fastidious?	**9**	_____
recounts a meeting of two strangers?	**10**	_____

TEXT A

Alex had the smaller of the two bedrooms. It was built into the roof of the house and had a restricted view of the dreary main street.

There was no double glazing for the window but the glass was spotlessly clean on the inside. The outside had a fine film of grime. Obviously Alex had no means of cleaning it off as the glass was fixed firmly in a fixed frame. Anyone would have been able to hear the conversations of the old people in front of the house and probably further up and down the street.

Alex was a young man, less than twenty-two, and his room was so functional and tidy the rare visitor felt compelled to make some vague but positive appraisal. A psychologist might be inclined to comment that it indicated a need for control—to be orderly. There was a three-quarter-sized bed against one wall, the bedspread folded back to exactly halfway to air the sheets underneath. Under the window in part of the room, where the ceiling was most low, a small desk held a small laptop. There was no printer. Probably had no need for one. Young adults nowadays communicate electronically.

From *The Glass Room* by Ann Cleeves

TEXT B

Nobody stopped me or asked who I was as I made my way into the foyer as I followed the signs leading to RECEPTION. As I got there, I noticed a small group of people standing just a short distance back from the high-fronted desk: two young men no longer teenagers accompanied by an older woman. The older of the two men was dressed in a suit with a grey overcoat. He had slicked-back hair and olive skin. He stood a short pace away from the others and was looking down intensely at his phone.

The younger was dressed in jeans and a jumper and had small round glasses and a beard. His jeans were dirty and his jumper was unravelling at the cuffs. He was bear-shaped and had a hand lightly on the woman's shoulder. She was dressed entirely in black including a small but unobtrusive dark head covering. Her grey hair was cut short. I wouldn't have been at all surprised if she had been wearing a flimsy veil.

She watched me sadly as I stood a respectable distance from the front desk.

From *A Death in Rembrandt Square* by Anja de Jager

TEXT C

Rip now felt a vague apprehension stealing over him; he looked anxiously in the same direction, and perceived a strange figure slowly toiling up the rocks and bending under the weight of something he carried on his back. He was surprised to see any human being in this lonely and unfrequented place, but supposing it to be someone of the neighbourhood in need of his assistance, he hastened down to yield it.

On nearer approach, he was still more surprised at the singularity of the stranger's appearance. He was a short, square-built old fellow, with thick bushy hair, and a grizzled beard. His dress was of the antique Dutch fashion—a cloth jerkin strapped round the waist—several pairs of breeches, the outer one of ample volume, decorated with rows of buttons down the sides and bunches at the knees. He bore on his shoulder a stout keg, that seemed full of liquor, and made signs for Rip to approach and assist him with the load.

From *Rip Van Winkle* by Washington Irving

TEXT D

He was at least fifty, and he looked it. His hair was long and tangled and greasy, and hung down, and you could see his eyes shining through like he was behind vines. It was all black, no grey; so was his long, mixed-up whiskers. There wasn't any colour in his face, where his face showed; it was white; not like another man's white, but a white to make a body sick, a white to make a body's flesh crawl—a tree-toad white, a fish-belly white.

As for his clothes—just rags, that was all. He had one ankle resting on the other knee; the boot on that foot was busted, and two of his toes stuck through, and he worked them now and then. His hat was laying on the floor—an old black slouch hat with the top caved in, like a bent lid. Except for a slight wriggle of his toes, it would seem most probable he had already passed away.

It was natural to want to step back.

From *The Adventures of Huckleberry Finn* by Mark Twain

Read the four texts below on the theme of chameleons.

For questions **1–10**, choose the option (**A**, **B**, **C** or **D**) which you think best answers the question.

Which text ...

describes a chameleon that has spectacularly accurate eyesight?	**1**	_____
refers to the hunting tactic of being a predator while avoiding being prey?	**2**	_____
raises the issue of a species of a chameleon being difficult to breed?	**3**	_____
reflects on how one chameleon species got its name?	**4**	_____
describes the writer as being impressed by a chameleon's overall appearance?	**5**	_____
states which chameleon is the least colourful?	**6**	_____
mentions a rare distinctive feature about a chameleon's facial characteristics?	**7**	_____
describes a chameleon with a taste for unusual food?	**8**	_____
explains the reason why chameleons are not like other lizards?	**9**	_____
discusses the special feature of a chameleon's additional eye?	**10**	_____

TEXT A

The Parson's chameleon is limited in distribution to the eastern side of the island of Madagascar (off the coast of Africa) and is native to the wetter forests. Chameleons typically live in hot, moist environments.

The King Kong of the chameleon world—nothing can match the mass and bulk of a Parson's chameleon—they are indeed the logical choice for the largest chameleon species in the world.

Parson's chameleons exceed 60 cm in total length at maturity, with body measures averaging 20 to 30 cm. This species may weigh upwards of 700 g at maturity. Parson's chameleons have a Pinocchio-like appearance due to the larger nasal appendages. Their garish noses make them easy to identify as a species. Males have been known to have forked noses or, very rarely, a pair of noses. Male colouration also is described as brighter or bolder than females. It's claimed they can be as big as a small house cat.

Males are larger than females. Males develop unique, jagged horns but females do not.

Captive-bred Parson's chameleons are very rare. The eggs are slow to incubate since they must undergo a type of hibernation period called diapause. It can take two years for them to hatch.

Adapted from http://www.pet-chameleon-care.com/chameleons/largest-chameleons.html

TEXT B

Meller's chameleons are big chameleons. They are, in some opinions, the second-largest species of chameleon in the world. They are a heavy-bodied species with a tall dorsal crest.

One defining characteristic is their 'nose' horn. Often this horn is bent or missing due to combative encounters. It doesn't grow back and it is unusual to see one fully intact in the environment. Unlike many lizards, chameleons cannot regrow their tail.

Meller's chameleons are named after an 1800s botanist and are the largest of the mainland African chameleons—the largest chameleons on the continent of Africa. They are also known as 'bird-eating' chameleons, which gives some idea of their size. Their big claws tend to be strong and can readily draw blood, much like the Parson's chameleons.

It's believed that Meller's chameleons can reach 75 cm in length and many say from personal experience that they're a very robust chameleon, tending to be on the aggressive side. It is an impressive species and beautifully coloured with greens, yellows, black and white. They can be quite relaxed in group situations, unlike most chameleons.

Adapted from http://www.pet-chameleon-care.com/chameleons/largest-chameleons.html

TEXT C

Giant spiny chameleons are a beautiful species of tree lizard found in Madagascar. They are normally found within the denser sections of forest where prey and cover are abundant.

This species has a lot in common with other chameleons. The males are quite large (55 cm) but less colourful. They are mostly brown, grey and green with a white stripe running the length of the abdomen. They can change colour slightly but this would normally just be to brighten or darken the existing pattern.

As with other chameleons there is a stark contrast between males and females of the species. Males are generally more colourful with distinctive patterns running the length of their abdomen. They are generally larger and longer lived than females. The females have a less prominent crest.

This chameleon is a brilliant hunter and can spot its prey up to 10 m away. They normally remain still on their branch with leaves in the backdrop to break up their shape. The eyes move individually, looking to spot prey then come together to provide depth perception when about to strike. It is extremely accurate with its extendable tongue and can catch many insects, amphibians, small reptiles and small mammals.

Adapted from http://www.pet-chameleon-care.com/chameleons/largest-chameleons.html

TEXT D

The Oustalet's chameleon, known as the Malagasy giant chameleon, lives a mostly sedentary life. It moves slowly, or not at all, for long periods. This conserves energy and enables it to stay out of sight of predators—and to be a predator itself. When an unsuspecting insect, lizard or small bird passes by, its extremely long, suction-cup-tipped tongue darts out to snare the creature. The tongue is spring-loaded and shoots forward like a bow from an arrow to nearly twice the length of the entire chameleon.

The Oustalet's chameleon has a crest of small, triangular spikes down its back and a long tail that it can wrap around branches, use as a counterbalance or simply curl into a scaly spiral. It has a third eye on top of its head, although this functions more like a light meter than a high-definition eye.

This giant of Madagascar can grow to 50 cm and clocks in as the world's second-heaviest chameleon. It's a solitary creature, showing aggression toward other chameleons via rapid colour changes and confrontational posturing. It was recently discovered to be somewhat omnivorous (not exclusively carnivorous) and munches on certain native shrubs.

Oustalet's chameleons aren't considered endangered.

Adapted from http://www.pet-chameleon-care.com/chameleons/largest-chameleons.html

MINI TEST 46: Narratives

Read the four texts below on the theme of dialogue.

For questions **1–10**, choose the option (**A**, **B**, **C** or **D**) which you think best answers the question.

Which text ...

describes a character feeling a sense of frustration with a confused friend?	**1**	_____
portrays a growing anxiety that something is amiss?	**2**	_____
mentions the state of a character's hair?	**3**	_____
depicts a character's naivety in an everyday situation?	**4**	_____
makes plain the character's scepticism about the value of goods on offer?	**5**	_____
alludes to a developing tension between the characters?	**6**	_____
depicts behaviour that would be considered inappropriate among friends?	**7**	_____
describes the features of a strange creature?	**8**	_____
explains the reason why a character was working in an unrefined manner?	**9**	_____
discusses some advice about table manners?	**10**	_____

TEXT A

We wandered along the garage sale tables. There were garden gnomes, old brooms and a used toilet brush, the lids off pots, some yellowing kitchen gadgets, heaps of old socks and underwear and yellowing electrical equipment. Not much that grabbed my interest.

Eve picked up a shiny plaster reindeer. There was a white gash where an ear had once been.

'Reindeer,' said Doreen, the seated owner.

'Rain?' Eve looked at the sky and frowned. 'Don't think so.'

'*Rein-deer*!' I said, pointing to the object in Eve's hands.

'Dear?' questioned Eve, looking at me disapprovingly.

'Not dear. All going cheap,' called Monty, the husband.

'Cheep?' Eve frowned again.

'Cheap!' I corrected.

'The reindeer. Not dear, cheap,' agreed Doreen.

We were starting to sound like a chicken farm. I felt like flapping my arms. Maybe someone would lay an egg.

'Anything take your fancy?' asked Monty hopefully.

'Don't think so,' I smiled, trying to ignore the toilet brush.

'Not the things young ladies buy,' laughed Doreen.

Eve then picked up an object that resembled a clock in a rather tizzy wooden setting. It looked like a cheap souvenir.

'Barometer,' nodded Monty.

'Barometer,' agreed Doreen.

'Barometer?' replied Eve.

Here we go again, I thought.

Adapted from *Uncanny Climate Change* by Alan Horsfield, Macmillan Education, 2007

TEXT B

There was a table set out under a tree in front of the house where the March Hare and the Hatter were having tea. A Dormouse was sitting between them, fast asleep.

The table was large but the three were all crowded together at one corner, 'No room! No room!' they cried out when they saw Alice approaching.

'There's *plenty* of room!' said Alice indignantly, and she sat down in a large armchair at one end of the table.

'Have some wine,' the March Hare said in an encouraging tone.

Alice looked about the table, but there was nothing on it but tea. 'I don't see any wine,' she remarked.

'There isn't any,' said the March Hare.

'Then it wasn't very civil of you to offer it,' said Alice angrily.

'It wasn't very civil of you to sit down without being invited,' said the March Hare.

'I didn't know it was *your* table,' said Alice; 'it's laid for a great many more than three.'

'Your hair wants cutting,' said the Hatter. He had been looking curiously at Alice for some time.

'You should learn not to make personal remarks,' Alice said with some severity; 'it's very rude.'

Adapted from *Alice in Wonderland* by Lewis Carroll

TEXT C

That morning Pippi was busy making pepparkakor—a kind of Swedish cookie. She had made an enormous amount of dough and rolled it out on the kitchen floor.

'Because,' said Pippi to herself, 'what earthly use is a baking board when one plans to make at least five hundred cookies?'

And there she lay on the floor, cutting out cookie hearts for dear life when the doorbell rang.

Pippi ran and opened the door. She was white as a miller from top to toe, and when she shook hands heartily with Tommy and Annika a whole cloud of flour blew over them.

'So nice you called,' she said and shook her apron—so there came another cloud of flour. Tommy and Annika got so much in their throats that they began coughing.

'What are you doing?' gasped Tommy.

'Well, if I say that I'm sweeping the chimney, you won't believe me, you're so clever,' said Pippi. 'Fact is, I'm baking. But I'll soon be done. You can sit on the wood box for a while.'

Pippi could work fast. Tommy and Annika sat and watched how she went through the dough, how she threw the cookies onto the cookie pans, and swung the pans into the oven. It was as good as a circus.

Adapted from *Pippi Longstocking* by Astrid Lindgren

TEXT D

While the two boys were whispering, both the girls suddenly cried 'Oh!'

'The robin!' cried Lucy. 'The robin. It's flown away.'

And it had—right out of sight.

'And now what are we to do?' said Edmund, giving Peter a look, which was to say, 'What did I tell you?'

'Sh! Look!' said Susan.

'What?' said Peter.

'There's something moving among the trees over there to the left.'

They all stared as hard as they could, and no one felt very comfortable.

'There it goes again,' said Susan presently.

'I saw it that time,' cried Peter. 'It's still there. It's just gone behind that big tree.'

'What is it?' asked Lucy, trying not to sound nervous.

'Whatever it is,' said Peter, 'it's dodging us. It doesn't want to be seen.'

'Let's go home,' said Susan.

And then, though nobody said it out loud, everyone suddenly realised the same fact that Edmund had just whispered to Peter. They were lost.

'What's it like?' said Lucy.

'It's—it's a kind of animal,' said Susan, 'Look! Look! Quick! There it is.'

They all saw it this time, a whiskered furry face which had looked out at them from behind a tree.

Adapted from *The Lion, the Witch and the Wardrobe* by CS Lewis

Read the four texts below on the theme of monoliths.

For questions **1–10**, choose the option (**A**, **B**, **C** or **D**) which you think best answers the question.

Which text ...

describes the effect of chemicals on the monolith's colour patterns?	**1**	_____
mentions the depth the monolith goes above and below ground level?	**2**	_____
refers to the utilitarian purpose a monolith has been put to?	**3**	_____
points out a world record held by a monolith?	**4**	_____
recounts an interwoven history between two cultures?	**5**	_____
states the geological difference between the two largest monoliths?	**6**	_____
provides an explanation for a monolith's original creation?	**7**	_____
raises questions about the significance and production of cave art?	**8**	_____
explains the reason for a monolith's colour changes?	**9**	_____
describes a secondary feature that contributes to a monolith's height?	**10**	_____

TEXT A

Uluru, NT Location: Uluru NP, 450 km west of Alice Springs

Uluru is one of Australia's most famous landmarks and is the country's most visited site. The mysterious red monolith is the weathered peak of a buried mountain range and rises some 430 metres from the desert and has a perimeter of 9.4 km. The rock is believed to extend several kilometres below the surface and covers an area of 3.3 square kilometres. The red colour of Uluru is due to iron minerals in the surface rocks oxidising with the air.

Uluru is also very notable for appearing to change colour at different times of the day and year, most notably when it glows red at dawn and sunset.

Archaeological findings to the east and west indicate that humans settled in the area more than 10 000 years ago.

Europeans arrived in the Australian Western Desert in the 1870s. Uluru was first mapped by Europeans in 1872 during the expeditionary period made possible by the construction of the Overland Telegraph Line. In 1873 William Gosse observed Uluru and named it Ayers Rock, in honour of South Australian dignitary Sir Henry Ayers. It had a name change in 1993.

Adapted from http://www.australiaforeveryone.com.au/files/topten_monoliths.html

---

TEXT B

Mount Augustus, WA Location: 320 km east of Carnarvon and 1000 km north of Perth

Though Uluru is the largest 'free-standing' monolith, Mount Augustus is the world's largest monolith. It is 2.5 times larger than Uluru. It is one of the most spectacular solitary peaks in the world, standing at 1105 metres above sea level. Its summit has a small peak on a plateau and rises about 717 metres above a stony, red sandplain of arid shrubland. The rock is 8 km long and covers an area of 4795 hectares. The mountain is clearly visible from the air for more than 160 km.

The site consists of sand and gravel that was deposited by an ancient river system that drained the region about 1600 million years ago. The river deposits consolidated to form sandstone and conglomerate, and were then buried beneath marine sediments when shallow seas covered the region between 1600 and 1070 million years ago.

Mount Augustus is known as Burringurrah to the local Wajarri people. Evidence of early First Nations Australian habitation is depicted in the rock engravings around Mount Augustus. Many Dreamtime stories of the Wajarri people can be viewed in the rock engravings in nearby towns.

Adapted from http://www.australiaforeveryone.com.au/files/topten_monoliths.html

TEXT C

Wave Rock, WA Location: Hyden, WA, 340 km west of Perth

One of Australia's biggest waves is also the furthest from any ocean—Wave Rock rises 15 metres above the outback plain. Over 2700 million years in the making, today it's a popular tourist destination. Fourteen metres high and 110 m long, the face of Wave Rock appears like a breaking wave ready to crash onto a prehistoric surf, now frozen in time. Wave Rock is part of the northern face of Hyden Rock. The shape of the wave was formed by gradual erosion of the softer rock beneath the upper edge over many centuries. The colours of the Wave are caused by the rain washing chemical deposits down the face, forming vertical stripes of greys, reds and yellows.

The bare rock hill is crowned by a construction of low stone walls to catch and divert run-off water. This provided the first settlers with a source of water for farms and the town for many years.

Ballardong tribes believed that Wave Rock was created by the Rainbow Serpent dragging her swollen body over the landscape after she had consumed all the water in the land.

Adapted from http://www.australiaforeveryone.com.au/files/topten_monoliths.html

TEXT D

Walga Rock, WA Location: 1000 km north of Perth

This huge granite monolith is 50 metres high, 1.5 km long and 5 km around. It is one of the largest granite monoliths in Western Australia. An extensive gallery of First Nations Australian art exists within a large cave in Walga Rock, making the site of deep cultural and spiritual significance for First Australians. Most probably painted with ochre from Wilgie Mia, the gallery features motifs that are predominantly non-figurative. One of the more outstanding motifs is that of a ship with two masts, ratlines, rigging and square portholes in the hull, a remarkable occurrence considering the site is over 300 km from the sea. It is believed to depict one of the Dutch ships that visited the region's shores in the 17th century.

Several of the paintings are so high above the present ground level that some form of scaffolding must have been used by the artists who produced them.

The rock is of profound cultural significance to First Nations Australians. The Walarri elders are the acknowledged traditional owners.

Adapted from http://www.australiaforeveryone.com.au/files/topten_monoliths.html

Read the four texts below on the theme of 'What is …?'.

For questions **1–10**, choose the option (**A**, **B**, **C** or **D**) which you think best answers the question.

Which text …

describes the manufacture of a product dependent upon solidifying gas?	**1**	_____
refers to the long-term misuse of an unsafe product?	**2**	_____
mentions an unintended outcome arising from the development of a product?	**3**	_____
argues that fossicking may have led to the depletion of a commodity?	**4**	_____
states than one of the commodities is a naturally occurring mined product?	**5**	_____
calls into question how a popular opinion of the product may not be correct?	**6**	_____
mentions the importance of readily available, cheap raw materials?	**7**	_____
describes a product that is a copy of something found in the environment?	**8**	_____
explains the reason why a certain product is a health-and-safety hazard?	**9**	_____
discusses a craft industry that developed into sophisticated manufacturing?	**10**	_____

TEXT A

Glass is a solid-like and transparent material that has numerous daily uses. It is made from natural and abundant raw materials (sand, soda ash and limestone) that are melted at very high temperature to form a new material: glass. At high temperature, glass is structurally similar to liquids; however, at everyday temperatures it behaves like a solid. As a result glass can be poured, blown, pressed and moulded into many shapes.

Glass manufacturing has an age-old tradition which dates back to around 3500 BC when glass is believed to have first been artificially produced in Egypt and Mesopotamia to be used as jewellery and later as vessels. Since then, traditional craftsmanship has evolved into today's high-tech industrial processes and the number of glass types and applications has multiplied. Glass industries use many production processes. However, glass first needs to be melted!

Glass melting requires two kinds of raw materials: different types of sand and recycled glass. These are mixed together and put in a furnace to be melted at around 1500 °C to form molten glass. This is then removed from the furnace to be shaped and cooled down.

Adapted from https://www.glassallianceeurope.eu/en/what-is-glass

---

TEXT B

Dry ice is made by liquefying carbon dioxide and injecting it into a holding tank, where it's frozen at a temperature of –78 °C and compressed into solid ice. Dry ice is the solid form of carbon dioxide which can then be made into pellets or large blocks.

It is generally accepted that dry ice was first observed in 1835 by a French inventor who published the first account of the substance. In his experiments, it was noted that when opening the lid of a large cylinder containing liquid carbon dioxide, most of the liquid carbon dioxide quickly evaporated. This left only solid dry ice in the container. In 1924 Thomas B Slate applied for a patent to sell dry ice commercially. Subsequently he became the first to make dry ice successful as an industry. In 1925 this solid form of CO_2 was trademarked as 'Dry ice', leading to its common name. That same year the company sold the substance commercially for the first time, marketing it for refrigeration purposes. It is used primarily as a cooling agent but is also used in fog machines in theatres for dramatic effects.

Adapted from https://cryocarb.com/how-dry-ice-is-made/

TEXT C

Asbestos is a naturally occurring fibrous mineral that can be mined. There are six types, all of which are composed of long and thin fibrous crystals, each fibre being composed of many microscopic fibrils that can be released into the atmosphere when used as a building material in construction projects.

Asbestos is made up of fibres that are so small you cannot see them. If asbestos fibres escape into the air you breathe, you might get asbestos fibres in your lungs. This can lead to various serious lung conditions, including asbestosis and cancer.

Asbestos is an excellent electrical insulator and is highly heat-resistant, so for many years it was used as a building material. However, it is now a well-known health-and-safety hazard and the use of asbestos as a building material is illegal in many countries.

Archaeological studies have found evidence of asbestos being used as far back as the Stone Age to strengthen ceramic pots but large-scale mining began at the end of the 19th century when manufacturers and builders began using asbestos for its desirable physical properties.

Naturally occurring asbestos is only a health problem if it is disturbed.

Adapted from https://en.wikipedia.org/wiki/Asbestos

TEXT D

Rhinestones are named after the sparkling quartz pebbles once found on the banks of the Rhine River in Europe. These pebbles had a high lead content, which enlivened the brilliance beyond most quartz stones. Sources were eventually depleted and imitation pebbles were created to mimic them.

In 1758 Viennese goldsmith Joseph Strasser perfected the composition of something called paste to create artificial gemstones as in Roman times. The process of blending the ingredients wet instead of dry for more even distribution had previously produced mostly coloured stones. Strasser was successful in producing brilliantly colourless paste, then furthered the intensity by adding metal powder to the underside of the stone, which reflected the incoming light back through the stone. These days, the term 'paste' will often refer to antique rhinestones.

Meanwhile Eastern Europe gem makers added lead to glass and called it crystal. Lead made the glass denser and less brittle, allowing craftspeople to precisely cut many faces.

Crystal rhinestones are the top tier of quality in rhinestone manufacturing. However, the general definition of rhinestones is imitation diamonds, used in cheap jewellery and adding glitz to clothing.

Adapted from https://rhinestonesu.com/blog/why-are-rhinestones-called-rhinestones/

45 MIN

Read the book reviews below then answer the questions.

Text 1: *Rudi Hooper's Super Pooper-Scooper* by Alan Horsfield
Publisher: Big Sky Publishing, 2016
Cover design and internals: Nancy Bevington
Category: Children
Pages: 62
Price: RRP $9.95 (pbk)

This book was given to Julianne Jones by Big Sky Publishing for review.

Despite their best attempts to be noticed, Morris and Rudi Hooper have never received much acclaim at their primary school. But this is all about to change when big brother Rudi grabs the spotlight for his rather dubious involvement in the local 'Tidy Towns' scheme. Much to little brother Morris's embarrassment, Rudi is now Sandbar's official doggie droppings ranger! As the Hooper parents' pride grows, so does Morris's trepidation. Will Rudi's gross new pursuit end in disaster, as Morris suspects, just when fame is finally within reach? Or can Morris get to the bottom of this rather messy problem before everything hits the fan?

I must admit, with the title of Alan Horsfield's chapter book, *Rudi Hooper's Super Pooper-Scooper*, I was expecting a book full of corny toilet humour storylines. However, as I settled into the book, I discovered it was a well-written story about family, siblings and town pride—plus dog poop—and I became a fan of Rudi Hooper, who cleaned up the mess that nobody else would.

Rudi Hooper's Super Pooper-Scooper is a book full of everything: problems, conflict, cheating, inventions, sibling rivalry then support, all tied in very nicely with a large dose of humour. Every child, person and dog will relate to this story. Everyone has seen that person walking a dog who, as the dog goes down into the poop squat, looks away, then charges off immediately afterward, not caring to scoop up the offending deposit left by the dog. Thankfully Rudi has a solution for the problem, and gains fans and fame almost in a good way and totally in a dramatic way that will have kids in fits of giggles.

Rudi Hooper's Super Pooper-Scooper is guaranteed to capture the attention of children. They'll be struggling to hold in bellies full of laughter from the opening pages of this action-packed book. Their curiosity to find out what happens next will become an unquenchable thirst. There is no doubt this book will be a go-to for a second read.

Text 2: *Pirates of Tahiti: A Tale of Two Ships* by Alan Horsfield
Publisher: EJH Talent Promotion, 2019
Illustrator: Nancy Bevington
Pages: 172
Price: RRP $12.95 (pbk)

For older readers
Alan Horsfield's new time-warp novel is inspired by his own trips to Tahiti as well as actual historical events.

Hawkins Botwright, who is in his first high school year, is about to board *The Seabreeze* for a leisurely cruise of the Tahitian islands with his teenage brother Sam and their parents when, without warning, he is transported back to a time when pirates plundered Spanish towns of the South American West Coast, taking refuge in Tahiti. How did he get here? Why is he here? And, more importantly, will he escape with his life?

As one might expect from a fact-based book about pirates there are a few scenes involving violence (including weaponry) and drunkenness (though probably very tame versions of actual events) that might make it unsuitable for some children (or better suited as a read aloud rather than a read alone). There is also some rather challenging vocabulary for the intended middle-grade audience. The story does, however, offer readers an extremely well researched glimpse into a place and time so far removed from our modern world.

This book will appeal to children—middle grade and older—with a particular interest in pirates and history. But any child with a thirst for adventure will enjoy the twists and turns of the plot as well as the many colourful characters they meet along the way.

Small black-and-white illustrations and a few photographs break up the text nicely. There is also a glossary of nautical terms and an illustrated guide to some of the sailing ships mentioned in the story.

Reviewed by Deborah Kelly

SAMPLE TEST 1

For questions **1–8**, choose the option (**A**, **B**, **C** or **D**) which you think best answers the question.

1 Which review(s) suggest that the book(s) are suitable for older readers?

A *Rudi Hooper's Super Pooper-Scooper* only

B *Pirates of Tahiti* only

C Both

D Neither

2 The reviewer is somewhat critical of *Pirates of Tahiti* because of

A its corny toilet humour.

B the inclusion of actual historical events.

C a few scenes involving violence (including weaponry).

D some rather challenging vocabulary.

3 The term 'hits the fan' is a euphemism for a situation

A that will suddenly evolve into an unpleasant incident.

B where everything seems to be going around in circles.

C where no-one is getting anywhere fast.

D which is not clear to characters in the text.

4 When the reviewer saw the title *Rudi Hooper's Super Pooper-Scooper,* she expected it to be a book that was

A exciting.

B humorous.

C offensive.

D smutty.

5 The second paragraph of Book Review 2 finishes with a number of questions.

The reviewer included these questions

A to encourage people to consider reading the book.

B because she didn't find the answers in the book.

C to improve sales of the book.

D to demonstrate her skills as a reviewer.

6 The reviews were written by

A Hooper and Botwright family members.

B Nancy Bevington and Alan Horsfield.

C Julianne Jones and Deborah Kelly.

D Deborah Kelly and an unlisted reviewer.

7 Which family, the Hoopers or the Botwrights, have the most family members?

A the Hoopers

B the Botwrights

C Critical information, which is needed to work out the answer, is not provided.

D Each family has the same number.

8 Four boys are mentioned in the two extracts.

What is their order in age from youngest to oldest?

A Morris, Rudi, Sam, Hawkins

B Morris, Rudi, Hawkins, Sam

C Rudi, Morris, Hawkins, Sam

D Morris, Hawkins, Sam, Rudi

SAMPLE TEST 1

Strange hair

There's a girl on our bus with the weirdest hair
That I have ever seen
Sometimes it's pink, or red, or black
And once it was even green.

She'll cut it in the strangest way
With bits sticking out at the side
And let it hang down over her eyes
As if she's trying to hide.

One day she coloured it all in stripes
With colours bold and bright
It was standing up on the top of her head
As if she had got a fright!

She's had it plaited across her head
Or curled like a circus clown
One day she shaved it off one side
_____(13)_____.

But today when I saw her get on the bus
I couldn't believe what I saw
Her hair was long and golden and sleek
And nearly reached to the floor.

I used to think she wore a wig
How else could she change so fast?
I'm not sure how she does it
Maybe one day I'll ask!

From *Alphabet Soup*, 2017

For questions **9–14**, choose the option (**A**, **B**, **C** or **D**) which you think best answers the question.

9 The narrator's reaction to the girl who travels on the same bus is one of
A amusement.   B horror.
C mistrust.   D incredulity.

10 The poet makes use of similes.

Which of these lines is a simile from the poem?
A As if she had got a fright!
B I used to think she wore a wig
C She'll cut it in the strangest way
D Sometimes it's pink, or red, or black

11 The narrator thinks the girl probably wore a wig on the day
A her hair nearly reached the floor.
B she had her hair shaved off one side.
C her hair was coloured with stripes.
D she had her hair plaited across her head.

12 Which of the following was **not** one of the girl's hair colours?
A green   B grey
C pink   D black

13 One line has been removed from Stanza 4.

What would be a suitable replacement for this line?
A It looks a real mess.
B And let the rest hang down.
C Has it recently been washed?
D Her head is not round!

14 The girl with weird hair would most likely think the poem's narrator was a bit
A inconsiderate.
B uneducated.
C old-fashioned.
D encouraging.

Read the text below then answer the questions.

Six sentences have been removed from the text. Choose from the sentences (**A–G**) the one which fits each gap (**15–20**). There is one extra sentence which you do not need to use.

Chameleons

Madagascar, an island off the coast of Africa, is home to some of the world's most exciting and unique animal species. **15** _____ These include the long-necked giraffe weevil, the colourful, cat-sized panther chameleon and the bright orange-red tomato frog! The latest to join this impressive list of exotic creatures is a new reptile species small enough to perch on the tip of a finger!

The two adult specimens, a male and a female, officially known as *Brookesia nana*, or nano-chameleon, were discovered in Northern Madagascar's rainforests by an expedition team. The male nano-chameleon measures 13.5 mm from snout to the beginning of its tail with a total length of 22 mm. **16** _____ The title previously belonged to the Jaragua dwarf gecko, which was slightly longer in length. The female nano-chameleon was much larger in comparison to the male, measuring an overall length of 29 mm.

Even at first glance, this was seen as an important discovery.

It is unlike most other chameleons. **17** _____ It also prefers to live on the rainforest floor, spending its days hunting for mites and springtails in the leaf litter.

18 _____

The scientists are not sure how the species became so small. In most cases, its miniature size is attributed to the 'island effect', where animals trapped on small islands tend to evolve smaller body sizes. However, the nano-chameleons were found in the high-altitude rainforests, which have ample space and natural resources for animals to flourish. The reptiles' home is at around 1300 metres above sea level. **19** _____

The nano-chameleons' family tree further deepens the size mystery. The closest relative of these newly discovered chameleons is nearly twice as large and occurs in the same mountains. That shows that this extreme miniaturisation has arisen independently in these chameleons.

Researchers, who were unable to find any more nano-chameleon specimens, believe the reptiles' habitat is most likely limited to just a few hectares. If correct, this could place the lizards at risk of extinction. Unfortunately the habitat of the nano-chameleon is under heavy pressure from logging deforestation. The area has recently been declared a protected area. **20** _____

Adapted from https://www.pet-chameleon-care.com/chameleons/largest-chameleons.html

A	It is the smallest among all the world's 11 500 known reptile species.
B	This is quite unusual for this group of miniature chameleons.
C	Hopefully that will enable this tiny new chameleon to survive.
D	The forests of Madagascar are where some of the world's giant chameleons are found.
E	Many cannot be found anywhere else on the planet.
F	They are blotchy brown lizards and do not change colour!
G	Their nights are spent hiding in tall grass blades.

SAMPLE TEST 1

Read the four texts below on the theme of horses.

For questions **21–30**, choose the option (**A**, **B**, **C** or **D**) which you think best answers the question. Which text ...

21   describes the various ways in which horses can move?   _____

22   refers to using horses as a forerunner to machines?   _____

23   mentions horse riding that would be impossible in real life?   _____

24   implies that a horse-riding style is reflected in social standing?   _____

25   states that one particular horse was considered cold-blooded?   _____

26   describes an attribute that gives the horse a greater range of gaits?   _____

27   mentions a mythical equine encounter?   _____

28   describes a horse that was bred to be ridden with a saddle?   _____

29   explains the importance of size for a horse to fulfil its purpose?   _____

30   discusses the attributes of a horse used for cavalry clashes?   _____

TEXT A

Gaited horses are also a light horse bred for riding but are best known for their exceptionally smooth ride. Horses have three basic gaits: walk, trot and gallop.

With gaited horses you get all that and more: the pace, the stepping pace, the running walk, the fox trot, the rack and the slow gate. A gaited horse is a horse that moves each leg independently. Doing so allows one foot to constantly be on the ground, allowing the horse to conserve more energy than they would while trotting. Gaited horses are used for travelling as they have greater stamina and endurance.

Historically, gaited horses were considered a 'gentleman's horse'. They were used for generals, officers, plantation owners and men of wealth. Today they are prized for their show-ring flair and smooth pleasure riding on the trail.

TEXT B

Light horses are the opposite of their draught horse counterparts. Light horses were bred for speed, agility, endurance and, of course, for riding.

If it isn't a draught horse, a pony or a donkey, then it's a light horse. Light horses are used for nearly every form of riding from pleasure riding to racing and station work.

A variety of horse breeds fall into the light-horse category. They can vary greatly in height, weight, build and colour. They all have one thing in common, however: they were bred to be used under saddle. They played an important part in military conflicts before war became highly mechanised. They were the lightly armed and highly mobile cavalry horses.

Some light horses are also considered to be a 'hot blood' as well. Unlike a cold blood, the term hot blood describes a horse that is high energy, easily excitable and fleet-footed.

Examples of light horses are the American Quarter horse, the Rocky Mountain horse, the Pinto and the Polo Pony.

SAMPLE TEST 1

TEXT C

Draught horses are typically tall, strong and heavy work horses. They were bred to pull and carry heavy loads, as they can pull twice their weight. Historically they were used for many things ranging from farm work to carrying soldiers in battles. Before the age of machines, these big animals were the big machines of the emerging industrial world for hundreds of years. They did everything from freight hauling to carrying armoured soldiers. They were the trucking industry, the farm tractors and the heavy haulers of the pre-modern era.

These horses are usually even-tempered and level-headed. They are labelled cold blooded as they are large, strong horses made for working, paired with a calm temperament. The average draught horse weighs over 725 kg, stands over 16 hands tall (160 cm) and can pull over twice its weight for short distances.

A draught horse or dray horse is less often called a carthorse, work horse or heavy horse. It is a large horse bred to be a hard-working animal.

TEXT D

Pegasus was an immortal, winged horse which sprang from the neck of the beheaded Medusa. It was tamed by Bellerophon, who rode it into battle against the fire-breathing monster known as the Chimera. Later the hero attempted to fly to heaven but Zeus caused the horse to buck, throwing him back down to earth in disgrace. Pegasus winged his way on to Olympus where he became the thunderbolt-bearer of Zeus.

Zeus was the supreme god and the protector and ruler of humankind, the dispenser of good and evil, and the god of weather and atmospheric phenomena (such as rain and thunder).

Pegasus was commemorated among the stars as the constellation of the same name. Its rising marks the arrival of spring and, in Greece, of seasonal thunderstorms.

Pegasus's name means 'of the spring'. This alludes to the steed's connection with sources of underground water. Hippocrates was the sacred spring of the Muses on Mount Helicon. It was said to have burst forth from the ground where it was struck by the hoof of Pegasus. A muse is one of nine goddesses, the daughters of Zeus and Mnemosyne, who preside over the arts and sciences.

Adapted from https://www.equinespot.com/types-of-horses.html

Read the texts below then answer the questions.

Text 1: from *Gabriel's Gruelling Gourmet Odyssey* by Alan Horsfield

The cat flap swung a couple of times—*whump, whump*—and then suddenly stopped.

Once inside, Gabriel's head swung left, then right. It was the same old familiar scene. His whiskers twitched. A terrible smell was still coming from the kitchen. It wasn't catnip!

ZZZzzzzzzz—ssssssshhhhhh—glop.

John was asleep. And the television prattled on. Four car chases, one plane crash, several sword fights against alien invaders and one ad that had been repeated four times in the previous ten minutes. Certainly not a smart TV!

Still John slept on, mouth open like a plughole.

ZZZzzzzzzz—ssssssshhhhhh—glop.

Val lay with her chin on her chest, in her favourite green chair. Her book was a deformed tent on the carpet beside her feet. The bookmark had fluttered against the cat flap.

John glopped and stirred. His newspaper slipped off his chest, onto the floor between the couch and the coffee table.

Time for Gabriel to move on. Retreat was the best option.

As John blinked and sat up he was hardly aware of the cat flap as it whumped to a stop for a second time in a matter of minutes.

'What's that, John?' asked Val, bleary-eyed. 'Is Gabriel okay?' She rolled her head about as if checking that it was still firmly attached.

'Errgh, ssssshhhhh?' was his groaned reply.

'Did Gabriel eat his food?' Val asked with some exasperation. She started blinking as if to check if her eyes still worked.

'Aarrgh?'

Now fully awake, Val asked, 'Where's Gabriel? Did Gabriel eat his dinner?'

John was slowly getting his bearings. 'Dinner? What dinner?'

'Dinner!'

An ad for weight loss caught John's attention. 'Yes,' he agreed, shaking his head to increase his concentration.

'John Andrews, did Gabriel eat his food? Did you check?'

John shook his head as he searched the black hole of his memory. 'Uh-huh. I'm sure he did. Has to be hungry.' His hands patted blindly for the remote.

Struggling up from her chair, Val said, with eyebrows raised, 'When all else fails, do it yourself!'

SAMPLE TEST 2

Text 2: from *The Rats of Wolfe Island* by Alan Horsfield

No thin plume of campfire smoke rose above the fronds of the palms that covered the island. Something was disturbingly amiss. Rex King, Kingy, would have heard the bus. I sighed deeply, then realised that I was standing in the middle of the road.

I looked in each direction, not really expecting to see anything more than a deserted road under a canopy of lush green.

The rattling bus that had transported me to this isolated part of the coast had disappeared in a cloud of dust and diesel fumes.

I crossed the corrugated road and dropped down onto a narrow beach. Wolfe Island was just across the lagoon. This was my third trip to the island. My first visit had been filled with anticipation and excitement, but now all I felt was apprehension and caution. I hardly noticed the tall, swaying palms and the clear skies.

I looked up and down the beach. For a moment I had the feeling that I was being watched. The feeling passed and all I felt was foolish.

I untied the little rowboat that was half hidden under some beach foliage, found the oars a little bit further into the scrub where I had hidden them and prepared for my short trip across the shallow coral waters to Wolfe Island. I bailed out some old rainwater that had collected in the boat since my last trip a month or so earlier before dropping my backpack into the bow.

Kingy's rowboat wasn't anywhere to be seen. That made sense. He would be on Wolfe Island.

My mind wasn't on the rowing but it was just a couple of hundred metres to the island. A narrow tidal channel right in the middle separated Wolfe Island from the main island. I struggled to set the boat on course for the opposite beach. It was only when the boat freed itself from the gritty sand that I started to relax a little and could survey the shoreline I had just left.

Behind a strip of vegetation was 'the road'—a coral-based track along the coast. I could still see the single-lane wooden bridge that I had just crossed before alighting from the local bus.

The road appeared totally deserted but I wouldn't have been surprised if someone had stepped out of the bushes and watched as I crossed the channel. It was uncanny how someone could suddenly appear.

All evidence of the bus's existence had quickly vanished. No rumbling, no black exhaust fumes, no cloud of fine dust.

We had hardly passed another vehicle on our trip out from town. This was well away from any tourist track. And this time I wasn't a tourist.

SAMPLE TEST 2

For questions **1–8**, choose the option (**A**, **B**, **C** or **D**) which you think best answers the question.

1 What was the narrator's strongest indication that the island was deserted?
A Kingy's rowboat could not be seen.
B the totally deserted road
C a feeling that he was being watched
D No smoke was rising above the palms.

2 In Text 1, when Val says 'When all else fails, do it yourself!' she is feeling
A exasperated.
B ignored.
C obliging.
D energetic.

3 Which person seems to be behaving most out of character?
A Val Andrews
B John Andrews
C the narrator of Text 2
D Rex King

4 Onomatopoeia is the formation of a word from a sound associated with what is named. In Text 1, which words contain an example of onomatopoeia?
A An ad for weight loss caught John's attention.
B the cat flap as it whumped to a stop
C I crossed the corrugated road and dropped down onto a narrow beach.
D She started blinking as if to check if her eyes still worked.

5 How many trips had the narrator made to Wolfe Island?
A This was his first one.
B He regularly made island visits.
C This was his third trip.
D The text does not give this information.

6 In Text 2, the author develops a feeling of
A exhilaration.
B foreboding.
C bewilderment.
D tranquillity.

7 Which character is most likely to be a bumbling person?
A John Andrews
B Val Andrews
C Rex King
D the narrator of Text 2

8 In the first four paragraphs of Text 2, we get the impression the narrator is
A feeling like a tourist.
B glad to be back on the island.
C becoming apprehensive.
D impressed with the view of the island.

The Singing Garden
DUSK
Now is the healing, quiet hour that fills
  This gay, green world with peace and
    grateful rest.
Where lately over opalescent hills
  The blood of slain Day reddened all the
    west,
  Now comes at Night's behest,
A glow that over all the forest spills,
As with the gold of vanished daffodils.
  Of all hours this is best.

It is time for thoughts of treasured things,
  Of half-forgotten friends and one's own
    folk.
O'er all, the garden-scented sweetness clings
  To mingle with the wood fire's drifting
    smoke.
  A bull-frog's startled croak
Sounds from the gully where the last bird
    sings
His laggard vesper hymn, with folded wings;
  And night spreads forth her cloak.

Keeping their vigil where the great range
    yearns,
  Like rigid sentries stand the giant gums.
On blundering wings a night-moth wheels
    and turns
  And lumbers on, mingling its drowsy hums
  With that far roll of drums,
Where the swift creek goes tumbling amidst
    the ferns.
Now, as the first star in the zenith burns,
  The kind, soft darkness comes.

Source: CJ Dennis, *The Herald*, December 1931, page 6
(Original title: 'In a Forest Garden')

■ For questions **9–14**, choose the option (**A**, **B**, **C** or **D**) which you think best answers the question.

9 The poet finds the arrival of dusk
A profound.   B dispiriting.
C unimportant.   D calming.

10 In which line has the writer used language metaphorically?
A Where the swift creek goes tumbling amidst the ferns.
B It is time for thoughts of treasured things,
C The blood of slain Day reddened all the west,
D As with the gold of vanished daffodils.

11 The flight of the night-moth could best be described as
A erratic.   B graceful.
C purposeful.   D methodical.

12 In the second stanza, which two senses does the poet rely on to create the atmosphere?
A smell and touch
B hearing and smell
C taste and touch
D smell and hearing

13 In the second stanza, 'his' refers to the
A croaking bullfrog.
B last bird to sing.
C lumbering night-moth.
D poet enjoying the sunset.

14 Which line is an example of personification?
A And night spreads forth her cloak.
B A glow that over all the forest spills,
C To mingle with the wood fire's drifting smoke.
D It is time for thoughts of treasured things,

SAMPLE TEST 2

Read the text below then answer the questions.

Six sentences have been removed from the text. Choose from the sentences (**A–G**) the one which fits each gap (**15–20**). There is one extra sentence which you do not need to use.

Twilight encounter

The setting sun gave a pink tinge, like watery blood, to the dark, cumulous clouds that sat along the distant, shadowy mountains creating an ominous, volcanic effect.

At Gate 5, within the perimeter fence zone, a sylphlike urchin looked up and waited. **15** _____ Feral strands of straight black hair hung across the smooth skin of her exposed face. Her thin brown dress gave little protection from the invading chill of twilight.

The square-jawed guard suddenly looked around. **16** _____ She looked up at him with timid, dark eyes. Her feet, in light, dusty material moccasins, were shuffling uncomfortably on the sharp stones of the asphalt apron.

She wasn't there an hour ago. He would have seen her when he did the security check. His first thought was that she had come begging for food—or warm clothing—but he had no idea where she could have come from. **17** _____. And dry spinifex grass barely covered the red drifting sands.

'Please sir, this is the Holt Surveillance Station?' she asked tentatively but anxiously. 'Please?'

The guard's brow wrinkled. His mind raced. There was no sign at the gate.

She stood well back from the fence. Must have been warned, Marvin reasoned without confidence.

She looked cold—but not underfed. Not begging for food. He realised he had a moral dilemma. **18** _____ But should he allow her some protection from the elements? Damned if you do, damned if you don't, he thought.

'I must see Dr Brice Cox,' the girl continued in a reedy voice. 'It's important, Sir. Sir?'

The guard grudgingly gave her his attention, more mystified than apprehensive, still baffled as to how she had materialised at his guard post. He looked towards the darkening ranges while he briefly contemplated contacting his superiors.

An impatient red warning light blinked annoyingly on a low, barely visible monitor in the guardhouse pod. He gave it a cursory glance then growled, in a slightly American accent, 'What 'cha want?'

19 _____

It made no sense to Marvin that a girl, about ten, could suddenly turn up in the middle of the desert and request to see one of the top specialists. It made even less sense as he knew that the presence of Dr Cox's arrival had been little reported on the base.

He shook his head. **20** _____ Could he send her back into the desolate land without food, water or protection?

A	There had been no rain here for at least a year.
B	Almost as far as he could see to the east was the low, woody, blue-grey saltbush.
C	Regulations stated no unauthorised admittance to the base.
D	A tightly held grey shawl was covering her head and upper torso.
E	There she was, patiently waiting.
F	She repeated her request, carefully studying his name tag: Marvin Kilroy.
G	An uncomfortable doubt niggled his brain.

SAMPLE TEST 2

Read the four extracts below on the theme of weather.

For questions **21–30**, choose the option (**A**, **B**, **C** or **D**) which you think best answers the question.

Which text ...

21 describes a weather condition not totally related to the elements? _____

22 refers to an example of extreme weather? _____

23 mentions the appearance of a deserted children's playground? _____

24 argues that, at times, being out in the weather could be a serious health hazard? _____

25 says the weather caused a change in normal travel plans? _____

26 tates that wearing a scarf would have been a sensible precaution? _____

27 mentions a place that looked obviously different after windy weather? _____

28 describes strange occurrences and features regarding rain? _____

28 explains the reason for a practical solution for trying to keep dry? _____

30 discusses the adverse effect of some city living conditions? _____

TEXT A

Rainy weather

The next morning I walked to school through rain that came down so hard it was practically a curtain of water. I abandoned the idea of cycling as I'd only get to the staffroom looking like a drowned rat. The wind pulled at my umbrella, fighting me for control and I had to hold on with both hands. Keeping it as low as possible above my head gave me better odds. My feet and the lower half of my legs getting soaked were the price I had to pay to keep my hair dry. It hadn't stopped raining all night and I had to jump over a puddle that was the size of a lake.

As I got to the pedestrian crossing before the school gate I sped up to a jog. The entrance was a welcome sight as I would finally be protected from the rain. I stopped under the awning and folded my umbrella letting a stream of water cascade down the fold grooves onto the soggy doormat.

From *A Death and Rembrandt Square* by Anja De Jager, 2018

TEXT B

Windy weather

I zipped up my coat against the gale that whipped cold air along the street. Where the wind hit the skin around my neck, it felt like it was stripping away any trace of body heat. My wife had told me to wear a scarf this morning but I had laughingly refused, taking on the demeanour of a scolded schoolboy. Now I was regretting it. She had been right. She often was.

The house on the corner of the road was overlooking a little park. In spring and summer it would be a pleasant place. It would be green and have small gardens of flowers. Today there was none of that. The trees were stripped bare of their leaves. The wind had free range and blew the empty branches this way and that. What might go back to being a lawn was now dead or dying grass edged with nothing but a trodden border of dirt. The children's play area off to the right was deserted. A metal chain swing tumbled and clanged with each gust of wind. The climbing frame a sad cold skeleton. All sensible kids tucked indoors.

From *A Death and Rembrandt Square* by Anja De Jager, 2018

TEXT C

Iron rain precipitation

Wasp-76b is what astronomers call an exoplanet, one that orbits a star outside our solar system. Scientists have discovered that the local weather conditions include 2400 °C temperatures, winds in excess of 16 000 km/h and a steady pelting of iron rain.

Wasp-76b, which is 640 light years away, is an ultra-hot gas giant. Because the planet is so close to its sun and is 'tidally locked' (like the Moon's orbit about Earth) it only ever shows one face, its day side, to its parent star, while its other side has a night side that remains in much cooler, perpetual darkness.

The extreme temperature difference between the day and night sides produces ferocious winds that carry the iron vapour to the cooler night side, where temperatures decrease to about 1500 °C and the iron condenses and falls as rain that constantly peppers the planet's gas surface and vanishes beneath it. It could be said that this planet gets rainy in the evening—except it rains iron.

It's a world we can't imagine easily because we don't have anything like that in our solar system, according to an exoplanet researcher.

Source:
https://www.usatoday.com/story/news/nation/2021/10/06/planet-iron-rain-could-have-hotter-climate/6017522001/

TEXT D

Smog

Smog is air pollution that reduces visibility. The term smog is used to describe a mix of smoke and fog. The smoke usually came from burning coal.

Smog was common in industrial coal cities and still remains a familiar sight. Today most of the smog is photochemical. This is produced when sunlight reacts with nitrogen oxides and at least one volatile organic compound (VOC) in the atmosphere. Nitrogen oxides come from car exhausts, coal power plants and factory emissions. VOCs are released from gasoline, paints and cleaning solvents. When sunlight hits these chemicals, they form airborne particles and ground-level ozone—or smog.

Ozone can be helpful or harmful. The ozone layer high up in the atmosphere protects us from the sun's dangerous ultraviolet radiation. But when ozone is close to the ground, it is bad for human health. Ozone can damage lung tissue and is especially dangerous to people with breathing difficulties. Ozone can also cause stinging eyes.

Smog can kill plants. Smog is also ugly. It makes the sky brown or grey. Smog is common in industrial cities with heavy traffic. In cities in valleys the smog is trapped and cannot be dispersed by wind.

Source: https://www.nationalgeographic.org/encyclopedia/smog/

MINI **Test 1**
Page 1

One text: Narrative
1 C 2 B 3 C 4 D 5 B 6 D

2 All options could reflect how Urashima feels but you are asked for a synonym (similar in meaning).

3 This requires a little mathematics and the need to read the text beyond the phrase 'tortoises lived for one thousand years': 1000 – 988 = 12, which makes C correct.

5 You are not actually told this but B is implied (see page 1) in the text and by the action of the Sea God's daughter.

6 This requires you to make an inference. You are not actually told what the Sea God's daughter's reason was for getting into the boat but D is the most appropriate option.

MINI **Test 2**
Page 2

One text: procedure
1 C 2 D 3 B 4 A 5 B 6 C 7 C

In this exercise take care with the times. Different times are mentioned throughout the recipe and it is quite easy to get confused under test conditions. The main difficulty could be with the cooking time (Point 3: 15 min.) and before serving time (Point 4: 2 min.).

3 The recipe requires 2 rashers of bacon to serve four people; to serve six people requires half as much again (4 + 2 people: 2 + 1 rashers).

4 This is a 'negative' question. These generally have limited use in tests. If a 'not' question is included, it will probably have the **not** in bold or capital letters to draw your attention to it.

6 Preparation time = 20 minutes; cooking time = 17 minutes; total = 37 minutes.

MINI **Test 3**
Page 3

One text: Information report
1 D 2 A 3 B 4 C 5 A 6 B

1 Check the prices. The Cool and Casual T-shirt is the only one that costs less than $40.

2 Alliteration is the use of the same letter or sound at the beginning of adjacent or closely connected words: Bold and Basic.

3 'Polyester' is a synthetic fibre, whereas cotton is a natural fibre.

4 'Accessible' is an adjective meaning able to be reached. The price is accessible to most people. It is generally affordable.

5 You read that Bold and Basic 'is also loved by the younger female'. It is not exclusively for men.

6 Check the text carefully. Don't rely on the pictures. The Summer Sizzler adds an extra layer of material under the main shirt for warmth in cool weather.

MINI **Test 4**
Page 4

One text: Information report
1 B 2 A 3 C 4 B 5 D 6 B

1 A perpetrator is the person who commits a harmful act. Bullying, in its varying forms, is considered to be a harmful, hurtful act. Criminals are often described as perpetrators.

2 Look at the first two bars of the graph. 30% of 12–13-year-old children experienced no bullying and another 28% experienced some bullying but none in the last month. This is a total of 58%.

3 This is a language question, As used in the text a suitable synonym for 'perceived' is 'considered'. The victim is considered 'to have less power'.

4 The answer is in the final third of the graph. 24% of the age group experienced bullying once or twice a month.

5   An accomplice is a person who participates in a wrongful act. The other three options are people who are not involved except by being present and seeing what has happened.

6   You need to look at the first two bars of the graph. 30% of 12–13-year-old children experienced no bullying and, of those included in the second bar, none had experienced bullying in the last month (but had experienced some in the past year).

MINI Test 5
Page 5

One text: Poetry
1 B 2 B 3 D 4 A 5 C 6 C 7 C

Narrator refers to the person telling/writing the passage/article/poem.

Especially with poetry, you should read the extract several times then choose the best option for the questions.

When doing exercises on poems do not always accept the literal meaning of words.

This poem is a little difficult if you take it seriously. The narrator of the poem is just another school student daydreaming, or fantasising about anything but school work. His daydreams are probably a result of not being particularly thrilled with sitting in the classroom.

3   The important word is 'really'. The answer is what is in the student's imagination.

4   We are not actually told what the teacher is doing—but ignoring the wild daydreaming of the student, she is most likely going about her work as normal.

5   This is similar to question 4 in that you have to find the implied answer. There is no sense of the student feeling bitter towards the others in the class.

7   The narrator believes that the students in the class would tremble with fear. He is not being realistic. It is unlikely the students would react as the narrator is really just another student.

MINI Test 6
Page 6

One text: Narrative
1 C 2 A 3 B 4 B 5 B 6 C 7 D 8 C

2   'Undisciplined' is best as it implies not really knowing how to fit in or behave in new situations.

4   This is similar to question 2 in that she didn't like her shoes because she was untrained (undisciplined) in conforming to regular school rules and had probably never had to wear shoes in the commune.

6   All titles have some connection with the passage but C includes the whole passage. A is out because the narrator did not join a gang, she **got** a gang.

8   A 'female Tarzan' would be athletic and resourceful.

MINI Test 7
Page 7

One text: Poetry
1 D 2 D 3 D 4 B 5 C 6 B 7 C

Don't forget: read the extract several times then choose the best option for the questions.

2   The words 'without sound' in the poem mean 'silent'. There is nothing in the poem to indicate that any of the other actions are taking place—even though they might be.

Take care not to pounce on the first word that looks as if it could be right.

3   Clouds, mountains and chart are all mentioned in the poem but, on close checking, none of them are correct.

5   You can work out the correct option. If you ignore the less likely options (strewn, trapped) and eliminate, in neat rows, (Crowds are never in neat rows!) you are left with C. The words 'random files' imply straggly lines.

7   The only beam listed in the answer options is sunbeam (A), which is incorrect. B (swinging air), though mentioned in the same line, is also incorrect.

MINI Test 8
Page 8

One text: Explanation

1 B 2 C 3 A 4 C 5 D 6 D 7 A 8 B

1 An emotive issue is one that relates to the emotions. This issue causes strong emotions in support of or against the eating of kangaroo meat.

2 The main purpose of the text is to explain the importance of a balanced attitude to kangaroos. The text gives arguments for and against eating kangaroo meat. The reader must decide where they stand in relation to the issue. The final sentence is critical in understanding this question.

3 The question mark in the title suggests it is intended as a question. It is to signal to readers that they should read the words as a question and that the text may provide information for the reader to answer the 'question' intelligently.

4 Cull has a specific meaning: reducing the population of a wild animal by selective slaughter.

5 You must read the text and **not** rely on the graphic alone. You are told the boxing kangaroo became an Australian sporting symbol in 1983 when it was used in the successful America's Cup yacht challenge.

6 The answer is in the text. Rightly or wrongly, the kangaroo and kangaroo-related marsupials like wallabies are considered cute and cuddly even if they are much too large (and wild) to cuddle!

7 Protected means prevented by law from being hunted. Slaughtered, in this context, means killed for food. The words have opposite meanings.

8 The picture portrays a multitude of kangaroos relaxing on a grassy field. Kangaroos might be unique to Australia but that is not the purpose of the photo.

MINI Test 9
Page 10

One text: Information report

1 D 2 A 3 C 4 D 5 A 6 A 7 A 8 D

Yolla is probably a new word for you. Do not let it distract you—its meaning is made clear very quickly in the text.

1 If you realise early in your reading that Yolla harvesting is as much a cultural activity as it is a commercial activity, many of the questions become easier.

3 Unique is a word that is often misused. If something is unique, there is only one of its type.

6 If Yolla harvesting has lasted for thousands of years, it must be well controlled (A). This information will help you with question 8.

MINI Test 10
Page 11

One text: Narrative

1 B 2 B 3 C 4 D 5 C 6 A

This passage includes: literal or metaphorical (imaginative) use of language, such as Q1 'Now I can die' and Q3 'silence to drown out the noise'. Some phrases are not meant to be taken literally. Refer to the passage often when answering questions.

2 Some questions will catch out those readers who rush in. There is a phrase in the passage ('there wasn't a Jew left') but the student should read on—'except me'. The correct answer is B, not A.

3 The silence of the neighbours has more significance than the screams of the woman.

6 This question tests implied meaning: you have to work out from the tone and subject of the passage what is really happening.

MINI Test 11
Page 12

One text: Narrative

1 C 2 B 3 B 4 D 5 C 6 D 7 C

5 The answer is suggested in the question. People, especially these Russians, do not have meetings so they can 'talk and argue' or 'listen

to tales'. They wanted to make a decision about trading with India—which had to be found.

6 This requires a prediction. Because Aphanasy was daring, it is implied that he would sail to unknown lands.

7 A daring person may do foolish things but he would also be adventurous. The text implies that Aphanasy would be more adventurous than foolish.

MINI Test 12
Page 13

One text: Persuasive text
1 B 2 D 3 C 4 D 5 B 6 A 7 C 8 B

1 This requires some common sense and a value judgement. Five-year-old children would be most interested in fairies and talking animals. The people organising the show are encouraging parents to bring their children (cheaper prices for family groups). Older children are more likely to go by themselves, if they go at all.

3 The show is only available on **one** day but there were three performances.

4 There are two shows per day for almost three weeks (no Mondays), which means just less than 20 days which is less than 40 performances.

6 The Bilbies have rhyming names so Dilby is not possible for a snake. Gaza Galah and Bettina Bunny are examples of alliteration (words beginning with the same letter) so the best name for a snake would be Sonia (it also ends in 'a').

7 Options A, B and D are not true. *The Bilbies* is a new show and therefore has not been running for years. The Pilgrim Theatre is one minute from Town Hall Station. The $38 special price is only for a family group of four.

MINI Test 13
Page 14

Two texts: Narratives
1 C 2 A 3 B 4 D 5 A 6 B 7 C 8 D

3 Hawkins has slipped back in time. The text reads: 'It was as if the Bora Bora Café had slipped back in time!' This point is also implied in the fact that he misses his phone which belongs in a later era.

5 A metaphor is a figure of speech involving the comparison of one thing with another thing of a different kind, which is used to make a description more vivid. Benito's grip was 'a bony claw-like grip'.

8 Over the duration of the text things get progressively worse for Hawkins. There is nothing to indicate that this will change.

MINI Test 14
Page 17

Two texts: Information reports
1 A 2 B 3 D 4 C 5 A 6 C 7 B 8 D

1 You need to know the difference between a geologist and an astronomer. Geology is the science which deals with the physical structure of a planet.

2 'The naked eye' is a way of saying it is possible to see something without help from binoculars, telescopes or microscopes. It is unassisted vision. A meteor shower could be seen this way.

7 There are only two planets mentioned by name: Mars and Earth.

MINI Test 15
Page 20

Two texts: Instructional texts
1 C 2 A 3 B 4 B 5 A 6 C 7 D 8 B

The small growing shoots of seed potatoes are called eyes.

2 Paragraph 5 states that potatoes 'prefer soil that is in a well-drained bed'. The 'bed' referred to is a garden bed.

5 Paragraph one states: 'Mushrooms are notoriously unreliable to grow, partly due to the mass-produced low-quality growing kits that people buy'.

6 Nonchalant means appearing casually calm and relaxed. The friend in Text 1 said, 'You throw 'em in a bucket, pile on the soil while they grow, and wait until you have spuds (potatoes)'.

MINI Test 16
Page 23

Two texts: Narratives
1 B 2 C 3 B 4 A 5 C 6 D 7 A 8 D

1 The characters in Text 1 are involved in a confrontation with a burly tree-lopper and venture into an unpleasant place. The narrator in Text 2 is frightened by noises he hears in the night.

6 Dusty's action of clenching his fists and holding them in front of his chest indicates he had a feeling of success. It is a common action of successful sportspeople.

7 The suburbs are cheerless (A). Text 1 states 'The streets looked more desolate and deserted but I'm sure there were people in the houses behind their drawn curtains. Some had grey smoke snaking out of black-rimmed chimneys'. Manicured gardens are ones that are cared for with precision so C is not the correct option.

MINI Test 17
Page 26

Two texts: Information reports
1 D 2 C 3 A 4 B 5 C 6 D 7 A 8 B

1 The expression 'give something the nod' means give approval to something (D). The researchers approved of the name reflecting where the fossil came from.

2 Flamboyance refers to the quality of being bright, colourful and very noticeable, including by behaviour.

4 The dispute over ownership is both legal and moral. The passage of time makes the issue of ownership unclear.

6 The Venus flytrap imprisons prey between two parts of its leaves. The two parts of the leaf then snap shut, trapping the insect. The sundew has sticky hairs that attract the prey. As the insect struggles to escape, other hairs close over it, holding it captive.

MINI Test 18
Page 29

Two texts: Explanations
1 C 2 A 3 B 4 A 5 B 6 C 7 B 8 D

First a quick look at tiddlywinks equipment:

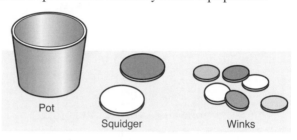

Pot   Squidger   Winks

2 A simile is a figure of speech involving the comparison of one thing with another thing of a different kind, which is used to make a description more vivid. The squidgers make the winks 'shoot off like projectiles'.

4 Ominous means giving the impression something bad could happen. Sliding down snakes can often lead to a variety of weird misfortunes. Of course, not all moves in the games have dire consequences.

5 Subterfuge refers to being deceitful. Tiddlywinks is not a game involving subterfuge.

7 Inauguration refers to the beginning or introduction of a system, policy or period. Here inauguration is referring to the beginning of the Tiddlywinks Club.

MINI Test 19
Page 32

Two texts: Narratives
1 C 2 A 3 D 4 A 5 B 6 C 7 D 8 A

3 Indolent means wanting to avoid activity or exertion; that is, lazy. Text 1 states that Rip made an 'escape from the labour of the farm and the household'. When away from the farm he would spend time admiring the scenery. As he left the hills 'he heaved a heavy sigh when he thought of encountering the demanding hassles of family life'. In Text 2 the father was protective. He let his terrified children cling to him. In the midst of the storm they prayed together. He wanted the family to stay together.

4 Vigilant means keeping careful watch for possible danger or difficulties. Text 1 states

that Wolf 'bristled up his back, and giving a low growl, skulked to his master's side'. He was behaving in a vigilant manner (A). Nonplussed means you are so surprised and confused that you are unsure how to react—this is not the correct option.

5   Rip was a malingerer. This means he pretended to be otherwise engaged to escape the duty of work: 'to escape from the labour of the farm and the household clamour of his family, was to take his gun and stroll into the woods'.

6   The text implies the correct interpretation of this phrase. The 'ship struck on a rock' and was falling apart: 'The shattered vessel was almost in two.'

MINI Test 20   Page 35

Two texts: Information reports
1 A 2 D 3 C 4 B 5 D 6 B 7 A 8 B

1   A clue is in the prefix *exo. Exo* means external, from the outside. An exoplanet is one from outside our solar system.

5   Both reports specifically refer to the likelihood of life on planets other than Earth. Text 1 states 'don't get too excited about the prospect of life' on exoplanets such as Wasp-76b: 'They can be hot enough to boil metal or locked in deep freeze.' Also the winds can be phenomenal. Text 2 explores the importance of dust affecting the possibility of life on a planet: 'studies strongly suggest that airborne dust can greatly widen the habitable zone on tidally locked planets'.

6   Text 2 suggests there may be life outside our solar system. Finding life (or conditions suitable for life) on a different planet is one goal for many space missions. Text 1 stresses the difficulties in finding suitable planets that could even support life so this is not a correct option.

7   Scientists are learning more about other worlds. In Text 1 we read: 'Exoplanets are worlds orbiting other stars and they come in a wide variety of sizes, from gas giants larger than Jupiter to small, rocky planets about as big around as Earth or Mars'. Text 2 is somewhat more optimistic: 'The universe is

an enormous place, so chances are there are other planets like ours'.

MINI Test 21   Page 38

Two texts: Narratives
1 C 2 B 3 D 4 C 5 A 6 B 7 A 8 D

Burlesque is an absurd or comically exaggerated imitation of something, especially in a literary or dramatic work. It is part of a variety show format.

1   Abbott and Costello's first rift was in 1945 'when Abbott hired a domestic servant who had been fired by Costello. Costello refused to speak to his partner except when performing'. Text 2 also states 'Martin became tired of scripts limiting him to colourless romantic leads while parts of their films centred on the antics of Lewis. Eventually they could no longer work together'.

5   The straight man is a character in a comedy double act. When a comedy partner behaves eccentrically the straight man is expected to maintain composure. Martin and Abbott were the straight men in their respective duos.

MINI Test 22   Page 41

Poetry
1 A 2 B 3 A 4 C 5 D 6 B

This is a very 'soft'-sounding poem capturing the peacefulness of the forest. Alliteration is an important feature.

3   Personification is a literary technique used by writers. Something non-human is referred to as having a human quality. 'October' is described as 'the maiden of bright yellow tresses'.

4   In the final stanza, the speaker refers to himself for the first time. The final lines state that he wants to use this peace he finds in the forest in his everyday life.

6   Wax in this context is a verb meaning get darker.

MINI Test 23
Page 43

Poetry

1 B 2 A 3 D 4 D 5 B 6 A

1 A nightcap refers to a hot drink taken before bedtime to induce sleep.

4 The mug is a very chunky mug—more the type of personal mug found in the family home. It is unlikely it would be used in a commercial establishment.

6 Several words refer to taste: coffee, tea, milk, hot chocolate, flavour. Even in the vernacular we may say (incorrectly?) something tastes hot or warm. Tactility refers to how something feels when touched.

A is the best option. Chemically speaking, our taste perception increases with warm foods, as opposed to cold ones, based on boosted activity of the microscopic channels in our tastebuds.

MINI Test 24
Page 44

Poetry

1 B 2 C 3 B 4 D 5 A 6 D

2 The word mill in this context is a verb. It means move about in a confused manner, without a focused purpose.

4 Try to visualise/imagine how you run when tired but determined.

5 A pavilion is a building at a sports ground with tiered seating.

6 The text reads 'At last there's a glimpse / of the sand on the beach / and the white foaming surf / is just within reach'. There is a sense of relief as the beach comes into view.

MINI Test 25
Page 45

Poetry

1 C 2 D 3 D 4 A 5 B 6 A

3 You read that Macavity wanders the streets unperturbed: 'He sways his head from side to side with movement like a snake ... You may meet him in the by-street, you may see him in the square.' He behaves very independently.

4 The power of levitation is the ability to rise and hover in the air, typically by means of magical powers. A fakir is a religious ascetic who traditionally abstains from all forms of indulgence.

5 Supercilious means behaving or looking as though you think you are superior to others. Scotland Yard and the Flying Squad are elite crime-fighting units in England.

MINI Test 26
Page 46

Poetry

1 A 2 D 3 C 4 B 5 C 6 B

3 The key word in the opening lines is 'remorseless' (never-ending). It may be dark (A) because of reasons other than night. The cold is often described as 'harsh' (**C**).

4 Clutches refers to a tight grasp—as if unable to escape.

5 To behold something is to see it. If it is grotesque, it is ugly.

6 This requires a prediction. C and D do not suit the mood of the poem. A is a possibility but B is more consistent with the giant's destructive powers. It is the best option.

MINI Test 27
Page 47

Poetry

1 D 2 A 3 C 4 A 5 B 6 C

Note: The writer of the poem was a First Nations stockman. Do not be put off by the unusual words.

1 The narrator is sleeping on the ground looking through the boughs (branches) of a tree. He can see the stars and reflects on the importance of the stars and culture.

3 Read the first stanza slowly to find what relates to each named star: 'There's Ngintu, with his dogs'.

4 The people of the Star Tribes have died (passed away) and their spirits are stars in the heavens.

5 The lines 'when you wake, you find / your swag, the camp, the plains, all white with frost' suggest the narrator slept peacefully. There is no regret but an element of

nostalgia. Nostalgia is a sentimental longing or wistful affection for a period in the past.

MINI Test 28

Page 48

Poetry
1 B 2 D 3 C 4 A 5 C 6 D

2 The phrase 'followed his nose' is a colloquial term meaning finding your own way by instinct. In this poem it has a different meaning because Bosley is actually searching for food using his sense of smell, which is better than the smell of tinned fish.

4 Bosley's owners were initially not thoughtful—they only fed their fine cat 'fish that came out of a tin'. When he finally returned they were over-indulgent. His owners 'give in to his every desire'.

5 This is a sequencing question. Read the poem carefully to determine the correct sequence of events for Bosley.

6 Wafting means passing gently through the air as some aromas may do.

MINI Test 29

Page 50

Poetry
1 A 2 A 3 D 4 C 5 B 6 D

1 The poet intends to amuse the reader not only by his observations but also by his overreactions to the situation and its outcomes, such as 'Last week in someone's place we saw / A dozen eyeballs on the floor'.

2 Affront means do or say something that causes outrage or offence.

4 Uppercase letters are often used as a literary technique to express strong emotions.

5 A simile is a figure of speech involving the comparison of one thing with another thing of a different kind, which is used to make a description more emphatic or vivid. A simile usually begins with like or as. In this line it is intended to be amusing.

6 The words 'HIS BRAIN BECOMES AS SOFT AS CHEESE! / HIS POWERS OF THINKING RUST AND FREEZE! / HE CANNOT THINK—HE ONLY SEES!'

indicate that children won't be able to function at school.

MINI Test 30

Page 51

Poetry
1 D 2 B 3 A 4 C 5 D 6 A

3 The poet is describing the coming of twilight: ' The rising moon ... Looks gravely o'er the ledges'. O'er is a contraction of over, a literary device used by poets.

4 Personification is the literary technique of attributing human characteristics to something non-human.

Placid means not easily upset or excited. The moon doesn't have a placid face. These are characteristics of a human face.

5 It is the water that 'leaps into the valley'. This is an example of personification. Water cannot actually leap like a person or animal.

6 The poet describes the base of the cliff as 'rugged feet [where] / Deep ferny dells are hidden' (dells are small valleys usually with ferns).

MINI Test 31

Page 52

Cloze exercises: Information report
1 D 2 B 3 C 4 F 5 G 6 E

1 D is part of the introductory paragraph about the text's subject.

2 B prepares the reader for the next two points.

3 'They' in the following sentence refers to tourists.

4 F provides an explanation of the previous text.

5 G contains examples of hazards which relate to the last word in the previous sentence.

6 E refers back to the word 'local' and the people of communities who know the mountains.

The unused sentence is A. While the idea stated is true, the thrust of the text is about the immediate value of mountains to people.

MINI Test 32 Page 54

Cloze exercises: Information report
1 F 2 C 3 E 4 A 5 G 6 B

1 This sentence supports the historical information in the introductory paragraph.

2 The second sentence begins with 'This', referring back to the 'five tonnes of rock material'.

3 This sentence adds to the description of ornithopods.

4 This sentence advises that the scientists may have options.

5 The word 'jaws' in the previous sentence is followed by a more specific detail about jaws.

6 'The spiky fonds of cycads' are examples of tougher plants that *Muttaburrasaurus* fed on, as noted in the previous sentence.

MINI Test 33 Page 56

Cloze exercises: Narrative
1 G 2 E 3 F 4 A 5 B 6 D

1 This is a metaphoric description of a road and track system across a city.

2 This sentence adds to the description in the previous sentence of the blocks.

3 This sentence adds to the description in the previous sentence of the fish.

4 The character continues surveying his environment—nothing moved.

5 The previous sentence talks about a meeting to come. B talks about the previous meetings.

6 The previous sentence states that the sun was rising. D describes the sun's rays.

The unused sentence is C. While the idea fits in with the mood of the description, it is not an important part of the subject.

MINI Test 34 Page 57

Cloze exercises: Narrative
1 B 2 A 3 C 4 E 5 F 6 D

1 This sentence furthers the description of the lid unscrewing.

2 The next sentence describes the narrator's reaction to the loud shriek.

3 The previous sentence tells of the crowd's general movement backwards. The narrator finds himself alone.

4 This sentence furthers the physical description of the Martian.

5 This is the beginning of a new paragraph. The narrator explains his mounting feeling of abhorrence.

6 The following sentence explains why the Martian had vanished.

The unused sentence is G. The passage mainly consists of detailed description; there is little opportunity for speculation.

MINI Test 35 Page 58

Cloze exercises: Recount
1 E 2 G 3 F 4 B 5 C 6 A

1 This sentence describing the route is explained by the following sentence that expands on the description.

2 This is an explanation of what had caused the first shadow which was alluded to in the previous sentence.

3 This sentence explains in precise detail a reasonably safe distance above the razor wire.

4 The ALL CLEAR signal would be heard on the young engineer's monitor.

5 This sentence develops the description of the bird's power that began in the preceding sentence.

6 This paragraph continues the description of the stalking occurring over the landscape.

The unused sentence is D. This is an irrelevant piece of information in the context of the passage.

MINI Test 36
Page 60

Cloze exercises: Explanation
1 B 2 F 3 D 4 A 5 E 6 G

1 The first word 'Another' follows on from the examples in the previous sentence.

2 This is a leading rhetorical question, to which the writer provides an answer in the next sentence.

3 This sentence mentions the effect of climbers on raptors. Later in this paragraph the writer mentions that researchers want to know about more than raptors.

4 Again this sentence follows a generalisation about bird habitats giving more information. The words 'Not only' are a clue to the fact that extra information is being provided.

5 This sentence is a specific explanation of the assertion made in the previous sentence.

6 This is a satisfying rounding-off sentence (a coda) for the article.

The unused sentence is C. It is implied in the text that no region is inaccessible to the determined cliff climber.

MINI Test 37
Page 62

Cloze exercises: Narrative
1 G 2 D 3 E 4 B 5 C 6 F

1 After hearing the dogs barking, Yuri ponders the rhetorical question which he answers negatively in the next sentence.

2 In the previous sentence Yuri stumbles. He then picks himself up.

3 The previous sentence triggered this unwelcome thought in Yuri's mind.

4 This sentence is the beginning of a new paragraph. Yuri is backtracking up the slope. As he gets higher he can 'make out the tops of tall riverbank casuarinas against a velvet sky'.

5 This sentence tells where 'the burst of barking' came from.

6 This sentence attempts to explain how long Yuri felt he had been on the run. He had no definite idea.

   The unused sentence is A. The night-time description may fit in with the general scene

but there is no place for it in the paragraph. It is repetition of information already provided in paragraph 6.

MINI Test 38
Page 63

Cloze exercises: Information report
1 F 2 G 3 B 4 C 5 A 6 D

1 This sentence goes on to explain why blood oranges are different from most oranges.

2 This sentence qualifies the importance of the claim in the previous sentence.

3 This sentence gives the reason for the claim in the following sentence.

4 This paragraph is about being environmentally responsible. The Council understandably wishes to ensure there is no waste.

5 These are spoken words, part of Benigno López's summation of the situation.

6 This sentence gives relevance to the facts in the previous sentence. It puts them in terms a layperson can understand.

The unused sentence is E. The scheme is already successful.

MINI Test 39
Page 65

Cloze exercises: Recount
1 F 2 C 3 E 4 D 5 G 6 A

1 As Peterkin and his companion(s) watched the penguins, 'They [the penguins] returned our gaze with curiosity'.

2 This sentence continues the description of the penguins, especially their wings. The description continues into the next sentence.

3 The following sentence explains why Peterkin and his companion(s) were stunned. The birds covered the rocks in thousands.

4 This sentence extends the description of the penguins 'going down on all fours'.

5 This sentence describes the behaviour of one big bird. It had run to the sea. The following sentence tells what happened next: it plunged into the sea.

6 One person had pointed. The next sentence tells what the others did. They saw a penguin walking slowly along with an egg under its tail.

The unused sentence is B. This could be true but there is no evidence in the text to support this sentence.

MINI Test 40   Page 66

Comparing four texts: Information reports

1 A 2 B 3 D 4 C 5 A 6 B 7 C 8 D 9 C 10 D

1 Ceduna is the answer: 'The service centre for a rural area known for its agriculture (predominantly grain and sheep), salt and gypsum mining and seafood—particularly oysters—Ceduna is set amidst a patchwork of grain farms'.

2 Woomera was purpose built: 'Woomera is an artificial town specifically designed by the Long-Range Weapons Board of Administration to provide accommodation and facilities for personnel ... who came to work at an isolated experimental station which was used to test rockets, weapons and missiles.'

3 Text D talks about Arltunga's history of the gold rush in the 1880s and informs the reader that 'Curious visitors can see pieces of meat safes, rusted wire, rusted cans and shards of broken glass littering the ground'.

4 In Mossman 'the trains bringing sugar cane to the mill actually travel down the main street (an unforgettable sight for visitors—very 'unspecial' for locals)'.

5 Ceduna is '1200 km to the east of Norseman in Western Australia'. This means Norseman is a great distance west of Ceduna.

6 Woomera was 'used by NASA and the armed forces of Australia, Great Britain ... Today Woomera township is open to the public. Its main appeal is the Woomera Heritage Centre and the Missile Park'.

7 Three of the four towns mentioned have a connection with First Nations Australian language or people. Mossman is the exception. It was named after 'Hugh Mosman who found gold at Charters Towers'.

8 Arltunga is a 'gold-rush ghost town' which means no-one lives there.

9 Mossman had a subtle name change, adding an 's' to its name: 'Mossman changed its spelling because of confusion with the suburb Mosman in Sydney'.

10 Arltunga is 'in the middle of some of the harshest Australian desert'. It has '40 °C temperatures ... [and] Limited water supplies'.

MINI Test 41   Page 69

Comparing four texts: Explanations

1 C 2 D 3 C 4 A 5 A 6 B 7 D 8 B 9 C 10 D

1 Johnny Appleseed 'made great contributions to the westward expansion of the United States. Chapman paved the way for countless new settlements around his orchards'.

2 Text D states that 'Mrs Smith knew the apples were not French crabapples and were distinctively different to any other apple she had seen. She had something very special.' Mrs Smith knew she had something important: a new apple variety.

3 These words from Text C provide the answer: 'Children's books about Appleseed have removed talk of alcohol from the story.'

4 Text A states: 'it turns out there are lots of great reasons justifying orchards'. It then goes on to describe these reasons.

5 Text A talks about the decline in the number of fruit varieties and the latest resurgence in interest: 'many customs and traditions have developed, as have thousands of different variations of fruit ... unique varieties ... were lost ... Luckily though, in recent years, community orchards have had a renaissance as people rediscover the benefits and pleasures of growing fresh fruit from trees'.

6 The second paragraph of Text B deals in detail with the detrimental aspects of orchards: 'Threats may arise from chemical leaching driven by over-watering, excessive or poorly timed use of fertilisers or pesticides, soil erosion, inappropriate storage of chemicals and disposal of wastes that can leach contaminants.'

7 The final sentences of Text D state that Granny Smith's apples had two attributes: 'Apples during this period were either categorised as being good for eating raw or best for cooking. Granny Smith's apple fulfilled both requirements!'

8 The first sentence of paragraph 2 of Text B points out that 'Orchards are a long-standing

and valued contributor to the wellbeing of the community and State economy'.

9 Text C implies that Johnny Appleseed may have enjoyed an alcoholic drink: 'Chapman's success was centred not around fresh apples but rather the cider they could create. Cider was a dinner-table beverage at the time.'

10 Text D states that Granny Smith's family was involved in farming during the 1830s. The family farm grew fruit trees and there were sufficient vegetables and eggs to sell at the markets.

MINI **Test 42** Page 72

Comparing four texts: Information reports
1 D 2 A 3 B 4 B 5 D 6 A 7 C 8 D 9 C 10 C

1 Text 4 states that the Eastern ground parrot was already an endangered species before these bushfires and so bushfire recovery is especially important. A captive-bred population may assist in recovery of the species after recent catastrophic fire events.'

2 Text A explicitly states that 'there were less than 50 orange-bellied parrots, including four females, left in the wild, but a large-scale captive-breeding and release program has managed to boost numbers significantly in a few years'.

3 Text B explicitly states that 'It has a unique territorial display where the male bird drums a large stick against a dead bough or tree, creating a noise that can be heard 100 m away'.

4 Text B states that the palm cockatoo 'has a very large black beak and prominent red cheek patches' and 'is a distinctive bird with a large crest and has the largest bill of any parrot'.

5 Text D states: 'Intense and extensive bushfire is a major threat to these birds.'

6 Text A describes the experience when some captive birds were released: 'The captive-bred birds took about an hour to fly from their aviaries. They did not seem to be in a hurry, stopping to eat bird food before flying away. The aviaries will be left open in case the parrots need to return for food or shelter.'

7 One adaptation of budgerigars is given in Text C: 'Research suggests they're better adapted to the harsh climate than first thought. Much like mammals, budgies can regulate the water they lose through their skin.'

8 Text D states that the Eastern ground parrot 'has a distinctive call, given at dawn and dusk, that consists of a series of piercing, resonating whistles, rising in steps, with each note flowing on almost unbroken, but abruptly higher than the preceding note'.

9 The words in parentheses in Text C provide the budgerigar's popular name: 'the word budgerigar (commonly abbreviated to budgie)'.

10 Text C states that the budgerigar has cultural significance as it is one of the creatures created by the spirits: 'the budgerigar ancestor also shines in the heavens of First Nations Australian astronomy and in Dreamtime storytelling'.

MINI **Test 43** Page 75

Comparing four texts: Narratives and information reports
1 A 2 D 3 B 4 D 5 C 6 A 7 B 8 D 9 C 10 A

1 Most of Text A suggests the room was in an orderly state. The last paragraph declares that 'The room seemed almost spotless'.

2 The writer of Text D feels disdain for the modern library. She says: 'The libraries they build now are horrible, all plastic sofas and carousels and paperbacks in protective covers. *Paperbacks!* And synthetic carpet on the floor with modernistic patterns that mean nothing'.

3 Text B emphasises the differences in kitchen designs and functions post 1960.

4 In paragraph 2 of Text D, the writer describes her pursuits more positively than the team sports some students chose to do at school: 'I spent many an afternoon there immersed in a pleasant fantasy horror while our first eleven lost another match to a cricket team down below'.

5 Text C explains the differences between attics and lofts: 'A loft is also the uppermost space

in a building but is distinguished from an attic in that an attic typically covers an entire floor of the building, while a loft covers only a few rooms'.

6   The writer of Text A notes that the bath was dry and there was a wrapped bar of soap. The room had not been used recently: 'How long since the owner had showered? Lisa wondered. The bath was dry'.

7   Text B points out that the changes taking place with the modernising of the kitchen are ongoing. For example, 'Floor tiles were yet to come!'

8   Text C describes how libraries in the past were places of peace, which is contrasted with those of today: 'Now it's just the staccato tapping of keys and the electronic warning beeps of impersonal devices'.

9   In Text C the attic has the following disadvantage: 'hot air rising from the lower floors of a building is often retained in attics, further compounding their reputation as inhospitable environments'. They are also described as 'difficult to access'.

10   In the room in Text A, Lisa found 'Over-the-counter medicines, remedies for colds and flu, indigestion'. These are personal items.

MINI Test 44   Page 78

Comparing four texts: Narratives
1 D 2 C 3 A 4 B 5 C 6 D 7 B 8 B 9 A 10 C

1   In the first paragraph of Text D, the writer describes the very unpleasant appearance of a character: 'a white to make a body sick, a white to make a body's flesh crawl'. He concludes that 'It was natural to want to step back'.

2   In the second paragraph of Text C, Rip describes the stranger's appearance: 'His dress was of the antique Dutch fashion'.

3   In the third paragraph of Text A, the reader is told that 'Alex was a young man, less than twenty-two, and his room was so functional and tidy the rare visitor felt compelled to make some vague but positive appraisal'.

4   The narrator of Text B is in the reception area of a building. The narrator 'stood a

respectable distance from the front desk' and respected the privacy of others in the area.

5   The first sentence of Text C records that 'Rip now felt a vague apprehension stealing over him; he looked anxiously …'.

6   Text D implies the writer suspected the observer of the other man could be forgiven for initially thinking he was dead: 'Except for a slight wriggle of his toes, it would seem most probable he had already passed away.'

7   The features of the place in Text B with 'the foyer as I followed the signs leading to RECEPTION' and its 'high-fronted desk' suggest the place was a hotel.

8   In paragraph one of Text B is a description of a neatly dressed older man. In paragraph two is a description of a younger man dressed in jeans and a jumper:'His jeans were dirty and his jumper was unravelling at the cuff ...'

9   Text A has many indications of Alex's fastidious nature. The window was 'spotlessly clean', the whole room was 'tidy' and a bedspread was 'folded back to exactly halfway'.

10   Rip in Text C supposed the approaching person to be someone of the neighbourhood but was surprised to see he was a stranger.

MINI Test 45   Page 80

Comparing four texts: Information reports
1 C 2 D 3 A 4 B 5 B 6 C 7 A 8 D 9 B 10 D

1   In Text C the Giant spiny chameleon has eyes that 'move individually, looking to spot prey then come together to provide depth perception when about to strike'.

2   The Oustalet's chameleon in Text D has a 'sedentary lifestyle' which allows it to stay 'out of sight of predators—and to be a predator itself'.

3   Text A states that the Parson's chameleon's eggs 'are slow to incubate since they must undergo a type of hibernation period called diapause. It can take two years for them to hatch'. This makes captive-bred Parson's chameleons 'very rare'.

4   According to Text B, Meller's chameleons are 'named after an 1800s botanist'.

5 The writer of Text B writes that the Meller's chameleon is 'an impressive species and beautifully coloured with greens, yellows, black and white.'

6 As described in Text C, Giant spiny chameleons are mostly 'brown, grey and green' and can only 'change colour slightly'.

7 Text A states that the Parson's chameleon, in rare cases, has 'a pair of noses'.

8 According to Text D, the Oustalet's chameleon can be 'omnivorous (not exclusively carnivorous) and munches on certain native shrubs'.

9 Text B states: 'Unlike many lizards, chameleons cannot regrow their tail.'

10 The Oustalet's chameleon is described in Text D as having 'a third eye on top of its head, although this functions more like a light meter than a high-definition eye'.

MINI Test 46   Page 83

Comparing four texts: Narratives
1 A   2 D   3 B   4 A   5 A   6 B   7 C   8 D   9 C   10 B

1 In Text A the confusion arises over the meaning of the words rain and rein, deer and dear, and cheep and cheap. In the final sentence the narrator had got to the point of thinking the confusion was going to continue: 'Here we go again, I thought'.

2 In Text D the group sees something they didn't recognise moving among the trees: 'no one felt very comfortable'. They talk in whispers and there's a suggestion they should go home. There is a growing anxiety. Lucy tried not to sound 'nervous'.

3 In Text B the Hatter comments rudely on the state of Alice's hair: ' "Your hair wants cutting," said the Hatter'.

4 In Text A, Eve is easily confused and doesn't know what a barometer is. She is rather naive.

5 The narrator in Text A checks out the uninteresting oddments for sale. She finds little that grabs her interest. The text suggests she is rather disparaging. She comments on the toilet brush and other items: 'Eve then picked up an object that resembled a clock in

a rather tizzy wooden setting. It looked like a cheap souvenir.'

6 Towards the end of Text B the conversation between the Hatter, the March Hare and Alice is becoming ruder and more personal. Alice points this out in the last sentence: ' "You should learn not to make personal remarks," Alice said with some severity; "it's very rude." '

7 Pippi's inconsiderate actions in Text C cover her visitors in flour: 'Tommy and Annika got so much in their throats that they began coughing.'

8 The group sees something behaving strangely among the trees in Text D. It was a 'kind of an animal' and had a 'whiskered furry face'.

9 In Text C, Pippi was making 'at least five hundred cookies' which she was rolling out on the floor. Her friends noticed that 'Pippi could work fast'.

10 In Text B, Alice sits down at the table without being invited. She is offered wine but there is none available. She and the March Hare discuss whose behaviour was impolite: ' "Then it wasn't very civil of you to offer it," said Alice angrily. "It wasn't very civil of you to sit down without being invited," said the March Hare.'

MINI Test 47   Page 86

Comparing four texts: Narratives
1 C   2 A   3 C   4 B   5 D   6 B   7 C   8 D   9 A   10 B

1 Text C states: 'The colours of the Wave are caused by the rain washing chemical deposits down the face, forming vertical stripes of greys, reds and yellows'.

2 Text A states that Uluru 'rises some 430 metres from the desert and ... is believed to extend several kilometres below the surface'.

3 Text C states that 'The bare rock hill is crowned by a construction of low stone walls to catch and divert run-off water. This provided the first settlers with a source of water'.

4 Text B states that 'Mount Augustus is the world's largest monolith.'

5 Text D states that the cave at Walga Rock contains 'an extensive gallery of First Nations Australian art' including an outstanding motif of 'a ship with two masts, ratlines, rigging and square portholes in the hull, a remarkable occurrence considering the site is over 300 km from the sea. It is believed to depict one of the Dutch ships that visited the region's shores in the 17th century'.

6 Uluru is the largest 'free-standing' monolith whereas Mount Augustus is the 'world's largest monolith'.

7 Text C explains that the Ballardong tribes believed Wave Rock 'was created by the Rainbow Serpent dragging her swollen body over the landscape after she had consumed all the water in the land'.

8 Text D discusses the reason for the inclusion of the Dutch ship among the First Nations Australian art and speculates whether several of the paintings are 'so high above the present ground level that some form of scaffolding must have been used by the artists who produced them'.

9 Text A states: 'The red colour of Uluru is due to iron minerals in the surface rocks oxidising with the air. Uluru is also very notable for appearing to change colour at different times of the day and year, most notably when it glows red at dawn and sunset.'

10 Text B states that Mount Augustus has a 'small peak' on a plateau-like summit.

MINI Test 48

Page 89

Comparing four texts: Information reports
1 B **2** C **3** B **4** D **5** C **6** D **7** A **8** D **9** C **10** A

1 Text B states: 'Dry ice is made by liquefying carbon dioxide and injecting it into a holding tank, where it's frozen at a temperature of −78 °C and compressed into solid ice'.

2 Text C states that asbestos fibres that escape into the air you breathe can get into the lungs. This can lead to various serious lung conditions, including asbestosis and cancer: 'It is now a well-known health-and-safety hazard and the use of asbestos as a building material is illegal in many countries.'

3 Text B relates how a French inventor noted that 'when opening the lid of a large cylinder containing liquid carbon dioxide, most of the liquid carbon dioxide quickly evaporated. This left only solid dry ice in the container'.

4 Text D states that rhinestones, once found on the banks of the Rhine River, were 'eventually depleted'.

5 Text C states that 'Asbestos is a naturally occurring fibrous mineral that can be mined'.

6 Text D states that crystal rhinestones are the 'top tier of quality in rhinestone manufacturing'. However, the general opinion of rhinestones is that they are just 'imitation diamonds, used in cheap jewellery'.

7 Text A states that glass 'is made from natural and abundant raw materials (sand, soda ash and limestone)'.

8 Text D describes how Strasser was successful in producing brilliantly colourless paste to create artificial gemstones.

9 Text C describes how asbestos 'is now a well-known health-and-safety hazard' because if inhaled the fibres can lead to various 'serious lung conditions, including asbestosis and cancer'.

10 Text A describes how glass processes 'evolved from craftsmanship to today's high-tech industrial processes'.

SAMPLE Test 1

Page 92

1 B 2 C 3 A 4 D 5 A 6 C 7 D 8 B 9 D
10 A 11 A 12 B 13 B 14 C 15 E 16 A
17 F 18 G 19 B 20 C 21 A 22 C 23 D
24 A 25 C 26 A 27 D 28 B 29 C 30 B

3 A euphemism is a mild or indirect word or expression substituted for one considered to be too harsh or blunt when referring to something unpleasant or embarrassing.

4 Smutty, as used in the text, is a word or description that may be considered coarse or vulgar.

5 These questions are called rhetorical questions: ones that require no answer. They are meant to encourage people to think about buying the book.

7 There are four in each family: two adults and two brothers.

8 Rudi and younger brother Morris are still at primary school. Hawkins has just started high school. He is younger than the teenager, Sam.

10 A simile is a figure of speech involving the comparison of one thing with another thing of a different kind, which is used to make a description more vivid. The girl's hair looks '[a]s if she had got a fright!' Similes usually begin with the words like or as.

12 This is a search and find question. The colours mentioned are pink, red, black and green in stanza 1, and golden in stanza 5. Grey is **not** mentioned in the poem.

13 In this poem the second and last line of each stanza rhymes. The option must end with a line that rhymes with clown. It must also make sense in the poem.

14 You need to make a value judgement to answer this question. The girl with the weird hair would think the narrator of the poem was a bit old-fashioned (even if the narrator is not). Think about the way older people react to young people's hairstyles.

15 This sentence gives further information about the subject of the preceding sentence: the animal species on Madagascar.

16 This paragraph is mainly about the chameleon's size. The sentence rates its importance regarding size.

17 This sentence goes on to explain why this chameleon is unlike other chameleons, which is the subject of the previous sentence.

18 The previous sentence stated where the chameleons spend their days. This sentence states where they spend their nights.

19 This sentence elaborates on the theory that a creature's size is relative to its location's size.

20 This sentence leads on to speculation that may arise from the information in the paragraph: that the chameleon may survive with the new declaration that their habitat is a protected area.

The unused sentence is D. While the fact is correct, the text is about nano-chameleons, not giant ones.

21 Text A states: 'Horses have three basic gaits: walk, trot and gallop.

With gaited horses you get all that and more: the pace, the stepping pace, the running walk, the fox trot, the rack and the slow gate'.

22 Text C states: 'Before the age of machines, these big animals were the big machines of the emerging industrial world for hundreds of years'.

23 Text D describes Pegasus, which is a fictional horse from Greek legend. It was 'an immortal, winged horse which sprang from the neck of the beheaded Medusa'.

24 Text A states: 'gaited horses were considered a "gentleman's horse". They were used for generals, officers, plantation owners and men of wealth'—people of social standing.

25 Text C states that draught horses were 'labelled cold-blooded as they are large, strong horses made for working paired with a calm temperament'.

26 Text A states that: 'A gaited horse is a horse that moves each leg independently. Doing so allows one foot to constantly be on the ground, allowing the horse to conserve more energy'.

27 Text D describes how Pegasus, the winged horse, was 'tamed by Bellerophon who rode it into battle against the fire-breathing monster known as the Chimera'. This is a Greek myth.

28 Text B states that 'Light horses were bred for speed, agility, endurance and riding ... They were bred to be used under the saddle'.

29 Text C states that draught horses were bred to pull and carry heavy loads: 'They were the trucking industry, the farm tractors and the heavy haulers of the pre-modern era ... The average draught horse weighs over 725 kg, stands over 16 hands tall (160 cm) and can pull over twice its weight for short distances.'

30 Text B describes how light horses were used for close contact battles: 'They played an important part in military conflicts before war became highly mechanised. They were the lightly armed and highly mobile cavalry horses.'

SAMPLE Test 2   Page 98

1 D 2 A 3 D 4 B 5 C 6 B 7 A 8 C 9 D
10 C 11 A 12 D 13 B 14 A 15 D 16 E
17 B 18 C 19 F 20 G 21 D 22 C 23 B
24 D 25 A 26 B 27 B 28 C 29 A 30 D

4 Onomatopoeia is a figure of speech in which words evoke the actual sound of the thing they refer to or describe, such as the 'boom' of a firework exploding or, from the text, the cat flap 'whumped' to a stop.

5 The answer is found in paragraph 4 of Text 2: 'This was my third trip to the island'.

6 Foreboding is a feeling that something bad will happen. The narrator feels a bit concerned that Kingy was not there to meet the bus. He goes on to say 'I had the feeling that I was being watched'. A feeling of foreboding is further intensified by the loneliness and isolation of his situation.

7 In Text 1, John Andrews comes across as bumbling. His newspaper slipped off his chest onto the floor. He sleeps while the television prattled on and his hands 'patted blindly for the remote'.

8 The narrator was becoming apprehensive. At first he was a little puzzled because Kingy was not around to meet his arrival. His feeling of apprehension is intensified by the loneliness and isolation of his situation. As he

says: 'now all I felt was apprehension and caution'.

9 The poet finds the advent of twilight in the bush brings a feeling of peace: 'Now is the healing, quiet hour that fills / This gay, green world with peace and grateful rest'. Exhilarating is too strong a word: it means making one feel very happy, animated or elated.

10 [B]lood, in this line, is a metaphor for the red sky at sunset. A metaphor is a figure of speech in which a word or phrase is applied to an object or action to which it is not literally applicable.

11 Erratic is the best word to describe the moth's flight. Erratic refers to uneven or irregular patterns of movement. You read about the 'blundering wings' of a night-moth as it 'wheels and turns / And lumbers on'.

12 The poet draws upon the sense of smell ('the garden-scented sweetness clings / To mingle with the wood fire's drifting smoke') and the sense of hearing ('A bull-frog's startled croak / Sounds from the gully where the last bird sings').

14 Personification is a literary technique used by writers. Something non-human is referred to as having a human quality. In this poem, night is described as a woman: 'And night spreads forth her cloak'.

15 This part of the paragraph describes the urchin standing in the cold. The sentence provides more information about her appearance.

16 This sentence tells of the guard's puzzled reaction to the girl's unexpected appearance.

17 This sentence describes the desolate isolation of the guard post which is extended in the next sentence.

18 This sentence explains in part the moral dilemma the guard is feeling.

19 The girl's response is to the guard's question. She repeats her request.

20 This sentence develops the discomfort the guard is feeling. He is torn between regulations and a moral sense of personal responsibility.

The unused sentence is A. Though the weather is harsh there is no indication of the possibility of rain. Distant cumulus clouds are unlikely to be rain-bearing.

21 Text D states: 'Smog is air pollution that reduces visibility. The term 'smog' is used to describe a mix of smoke and fog. The smoke usually came from burning coal'. This is a weather-type event caused by human activity rather than the elements.

22 Text C describes extreme weather on Wasp-76b, which is an ultra-hot, distant, gas-giant planet: 'The extreme temperature difference between the day and night sides produces ferocious winds that carry the iron vapour to the cooler night side, where temperatures decrease to about 1500 °C.'

23 Text B states: 'The children's play area off to the right was deserted. The climbing frame a sad cold skeleton. All sensible kids tucked indoors'.

24 Text D states: 'when ozone is close to the ground, it is bad for human health. Ozone can damage lung tissue and is especially dangerous to people with breathing difficulties. Ozone can cause stinging eyes'.

25 Text A states: 'The next morning I walked to school through rain that came down so hard it was practically a curtain of water. I abandoned the idea of cycling as I'd only get to the staffroom looking like a drowned rat'.

26 Text B states: 'My wife had told me to wear a scarf this morning but I had laughingly refused'.

27 Text B states: 'In spring and summer it would be a pleasant place ... Today there was none of that. The trees were stripped bare of their leaves'.

28 Paragraph three of Text C explains how a solid, such as iron, can become rain. The temperature is so high the iron melts.

29 Text A describes how the wind tried to rip the narrator's umbrella away. In an attempt to keep at least her hair dry the narrator says: 'My feet and the lower half of my legs getting soaked were the price I had to pay to keep my hair dry'.

30 Text D states: 'Smog is common in industrial cities with heavy traffic. In cities in valleys the smog is trapped and cannot be dispersed by wind'.

NOTES

NOTES